CONTENTS

INTRODUCTION

Do you ever feel surrounded by stuff? Like when you look around a huge store with floor-to-ceiling shelves filled with stuff? Or, in your own room, enclosed by stuff? Everywhere … stuff.

Picture your neighborhood on garbage collection day. Are the streets overflowing with trash cans and recycling bins? Do you wonder what happens to all the stuff that gets thrown away? Or maybe you've never thought too much about it. The garbage gets collected and that's the end.

But, of course, that's not the end. Whether it's new in the store or trash in the bin, everything is part of a life cycle, from harvesting raw materials to manufacturing, packaging, transporting and selling to using and consuming and, finally, to trashing or recycling.

This book is about the waste cycle — the trashing or recycling stage — and how we get there and what we can do about it.

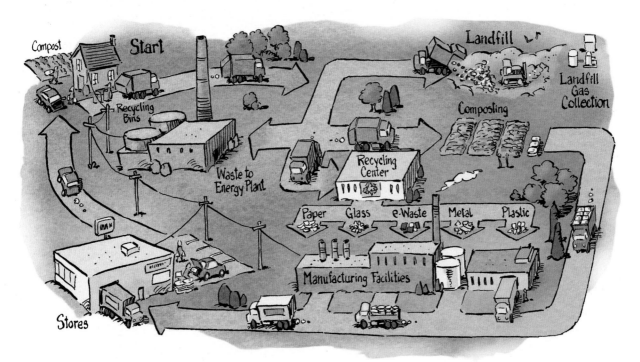

Your World in a Backpack

Do you carry a backpack to school? If you think about it, a backpack can hold almost everything we need to survive and communicate: water, food, clothing, paper and perhaps an electronic communication device.

In every chapter of this book (except when we visit outer space) we're going to take a look at something you might carry in your backpack to school. We'll see how it is produced, and what happens to it when it becomes waste.

Trash Talk

When it comes to trash, there's a lot to talk about. Some estimates suggest that every one of us will produce *600 times our own weight in waste* over the course of our lifetimes.

But all that talk also includes what innovators see when they look at waste. They look at water in the toilet and say, "Mmm, drinking water!" They see animal poo at the zoo and say, "Excellent! There's more fuel!" Scientists and students and regular people the world over are coming up with new ways to harness the power of waste every day.

Open-Loop versus Closed-Loop Systems

When we buy something, use it and throw it away, that's what we call an *open-loop system*. Objects are just discarded with no new purpose. For a long time, that was considered no big deal. There were fewer of us on the planet, and we had tons of resources to use and endless space to dump the waste.

Now, however, that's not the case. Because of our new awareness, the future of waste will include more *closed-loop systems*. That means that the end is just a new beginning.

For example, in a closed-loop system, recycling can turn a used aluminum can into a new can. The heat created from running a recycling facility can be captured and used to heat the building. And when you design something to be reused instead of trashed or recycled, the waste savings are huge!

The recycling logo represents the continuing life cycle of a product. It is an endless loop, never causing waste. The logo was designed by Gary Anderson in 1970 when he was a student at the University of Southern California. He won a contest sponsored by the Container Corporation of America. His symbol is now universally recognized.

Supply and Demand

You may have heard the term *supply and demand*. Let's say everyone in your class of 20 students wants to own this book. (Totally understandable.) That's *demand*. But the store has only 10 copies. That's *supply*. In this example, demand exceeds supply.

The rules of supply and demand apply to water, paper, metal — everything around you. The trick is to balance our personal wants and needs with the world's supply. Each chapter in this book ends with a look at supply and demand and what you can do to reduce, reuse or recycle waste. Sometimes you can change the world simply by changing your demands.

More and more we're learning how what we buy, use and throw away affects the planet. The great news is that you're reading this book! That means that you care about waste and want to learn more. (Or some adult is standing nearby and you want to look like you care.) Either way, keep reading …

WATER

Do you have a reusable water bottle in your backpack that you fill at home or at school? Beyond the tap and water fountain, where does that water begin? Where does it end?

The Water Cycle

It may seem that when it rains, water comes from an endless supply in space. But rain is part of the water cycle here on Earth. The water cycle, also called the hydrologic cycle, recycles the same water over and over.

1 **Evaporation:** The sun provides heat energy. The sun evaporates water from the oceans, lakes, rivers and streams. It becomes water vapor.

2 **Transpiration:** Water also evaporates from the leaves of plants.

3 **Condensation:** Water vapor rises into the atmosphere, where the air is colder. There, the water vapor condenses into clouds.

4 **Precipitation:** Air currents move clouds around the Earth. Water droplets form inside clouds. Droplets fall to Earth as rain and snow — precipitation.

5 **Collection:** Rain, melted ice and snow flow into the ground and waterways.

Water older than the sun?

Scientists think water may be even older than the sun. Why? They have tested water for clues. The formula for water is H_2O, which means two hydrogen atoms are bonded to one oxygen atom. But some water molecules also contain an extra molecule called deuterium.

Deuterium water exists on other planets and moons and in small parts on Earth. How did it get here? Scientists think it may have traveled in a giant cloud across the solar system before the sun began to burn 4.6 billion years ago.

Tastes pretty fresh for water that's billions of years old, doesn't it?!

Where on Earth Is Our Water?

Earth's water:

Salt water
97%

Fresh water
3%

Fresh water:
- 79% frozen in ice caps and glaciers
- 20% groundwater
- 1% surface water

Only 3 percent of Earth's total water is fresh water. We need fresh water for drinking.

Most drinking water is tap water and it comes from *surface water* or *groundwater*. Rivers, lakes and *reservoirs* are surface water, easily accessible to us. Water pumped from wells drilled into *aquifers* is groundwater.

What's an aquifer?

Picture a dog at the beach digging a hole in the sand. If the dog digs deep enough, it will hit water. This water comes from an aquifer — a layer of rock that water can seep through. The groundwater comes to the surface either naturally, as in a spring, or by being pumped up to the surface, as in a well.

Don't Drink the Salt Water!

If 97 percent of our water comes from oceans and seas, it makes sense to investigate drinking that water. Ocean water is *saline*, though, which means it has a high concentration of salt in it. Drinking it would make us sick.

Desalination is the process of removing salt from water.

For years, people boiled the salt from water using evaporation or distillation. Now, water is forced through cartridges that trap the salt, in a process called *reverse osmosis.*

The not-great news:
- Reverse osmosis requires a lot of energy.
- The salty sludge left over could affect delicate ecosystems in the ocean or ground (like if you poured a pile of salt into your soup — it just wouldn't taste right).

The better news:
- In nature, rain falls to the ground, collecting and dissolving minerals. The heat energy of the sun evaporates the water and leaves the salt behind. Scientists are working on desalination systems that use solar panels to copy nature's own process.

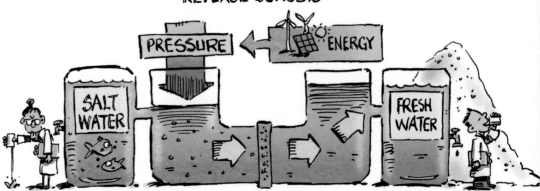

REVERSE OSMOSIS

PRESSURE ← ENERGY

SALT WATER

FRESH WATER

From Source to Tap to You ...

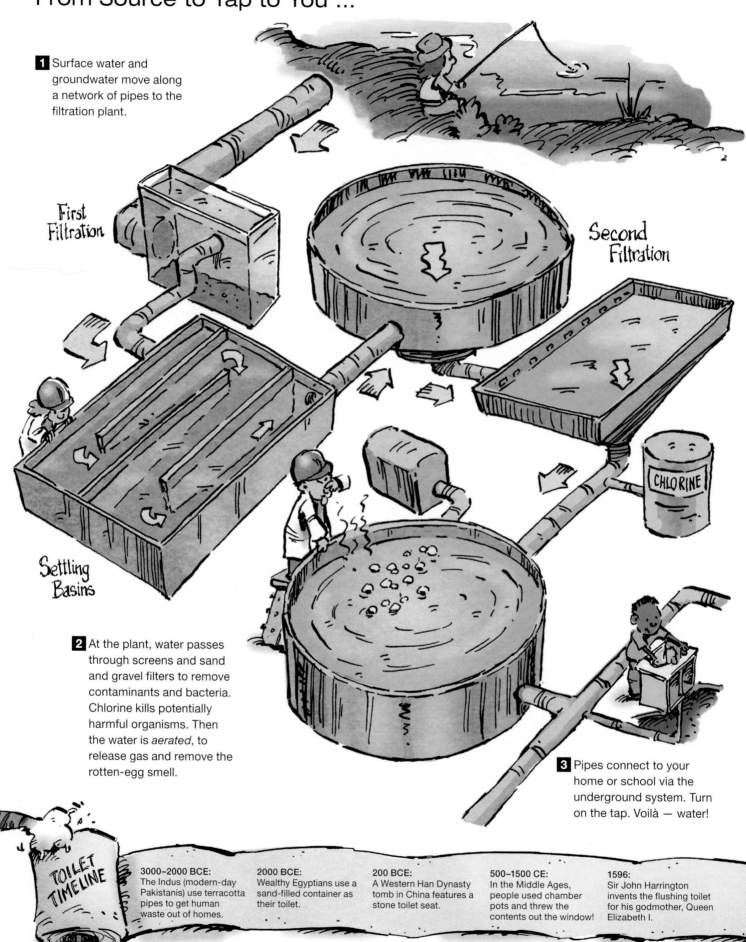

1 Surface water and groundwater move along a network of pipes to the filtration plant.

First Filtration

Second Filtration

Settling Basins

CHLORINE

2 At the plant, water passes through screens and sand and gravel filters to remove contaminants and bacteria. Chlorine kills potentially harmful organisms. Then the water is *aerated*, to release gas and remove the rotten-egg smell.

3 Pipes connect to your home or school via the underground system. Turn on the tap. Voilà — water!

TOILET TIMELINE

3000–2000 BCE:
The Indus (modern-day Pakistanis) use terracotta pipes to get human waste out of homes.

2000 BCE:
Wealthy Egyptians use a sand-filled container as their toilet.

200 BCE:
A Western Han Dynasty tomb in China features a stone toilet seat.

500–1500 CE:
In the Middle Ages, people used chamber pots and threw the contents out the window!

1596:
Sir John Harrington invents the flushing toilet for his godmother, Queen Elizabeth I.

... to Down the Drain

What happens to water that goes down the drain? It gets a new name: wastewater.

The wastewater journey is like the tap-water trip in reverse.

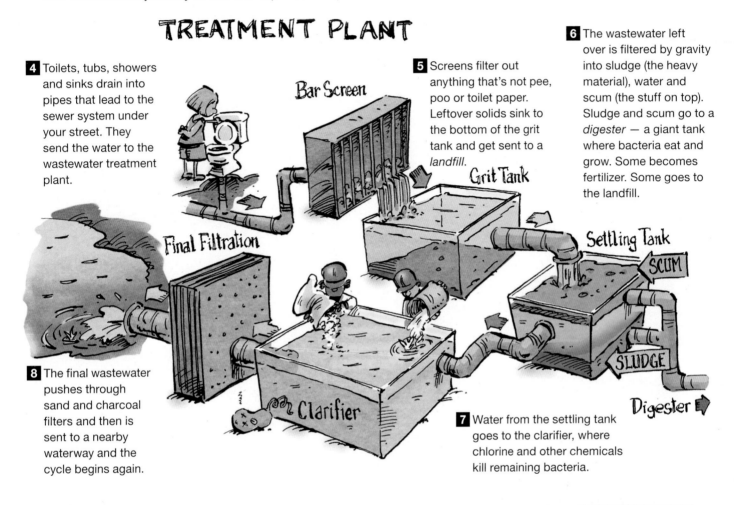

TREATMENT PLANT

4 Toilets, tubs, showers and sinks drain into pipes that lead to the sewer system under your street. They send the water to the wastewater treatment plant.

5 Screens filter out anything that's not pee, poo or toilet paper. Leftover solids sink to the bottom of the grit tank and get sent to a *landfill*.

6 The wastewater left over is filtered by gravity into sludge (the heavy material), water and scum (the stuff on top). Sludge and scum go to a *digester* — a giant tank where bacteria eat and grow. Some becomes fertilizer. Some goes to the landfill.

8 The final wastewater pushes through sand and charcoal filters and then is sent to a nearby waterway and the cycle begins again.

7 Water from the settling tank goes to the clarifier, where chlorine and other chemicals kill remaining bacteria.

Bar Screen · *Grit Tank* · *Settling Tank* · SCUM · SLUDGE · *Digester* · *Clarifier* · *Final Filtration*

Wells and Septic Systems

Many homes in rural communities use wells to get their water directly from underground, and septic systems to dispose of wastewater.

Some wells are dug and others are drilled. Wells can be 9 m (30 ft.) to 600 m (2000 ft.) deep, depending on the aquifer. Well water is tested to make sure it's free from bacteria and chemicals. When a well goes dry, it can take thousands of years to restore the water.

Septic systems use a tank made of concrete or steel buried in the ground. Wastewater flows through the tank into a drain field, where pipes with holes are buried in gravel. The ground absorbs the wastewater.

Never place a well too close to a septic system, or vice versa!

Q. What's the difference between *gray water* and *black water*?
A. Gray water is drained from sinks, showers, bathtubs and washing machines. Some people reuse gray water in their gardens. Black water comes from toilets. You wave black water goodbye when you flush, but scientists are working on recycling it.

1850: "Earth closets" are used. Pull a lever and clay covers the contents of the pan.

1890: Toilet paper rolls are invented. #gratitude

1910: The modern toilet with a closed tank starts to be used.

1992: Low-flush toilets become available. Using one saves 49 000 L (13 000 gal.) of water per year.

Today: At least 2.5 billion people don't have access to sanitary toilets. And many don't have toilet paper.

Tomorrow: Scientists are creating a toilet that recycles wastewater into drinking water. Yes, it's true!

You Want Me to Drink *What*?

With the growing world population, scientists are working hard to ensure there's enough drinking water for everyone.

Remember the wastewater journey? After the sludge goes through the digester, the remaining solid material is sent to a landfill. Instead of dumping it, what if we could use that material to rebuild our water supply?

Today, sewage treatment systems are being developed to deal with that waste without creating more. They turn wastewater into drinking water.

1 Sewage is collected and boiled.

2 Leftover sludge is dried and burned.

3 Water vapor runs through a cleaning system to make it drinkable.

Drinking Water

4 From toilet to tap! Cheers!

A Billboard That Produces Water

Almost 10 million people live in Lima, Peru. Most residents get their water from the Rímac River, but it's difficult to meet demand. Many struggle to get drinking water.

Also, this region doesn't get a lot of rain. Precipitation is almost zero. But moisture in the air (humidity) is close to 98 percent.

Students at the University of Engineering and Technology wondered: *Could they produce drinking water out of the air?*

They built a billboard with five generators behind it to capture the humidity. Water droplets from the air go through a reverse-osmosis system (like the desalination process) inside the billboard. The water filters into large tanks below.

Success! The billboard now supplies water for hundreds of families every month.

A Community Swimming Pool Heated with Wastewater

Treating wastewater uses lots of energy and generates heat. Scientists wondered: *Could wastewater help heat pool water?*

In Victoria, British Columbia, this question was put to the test with a heat-recovery system.

Wastewater flowing into the treatment plant is about 13°C (55°F). The heat-recovery system uses *thermal energy*. It captures the heat generated when treating the waste. That heat is pumped to the Panorama Recreation Centre next door, where it warms the pool water.

This closed-loop system allows the wastewater to be treated and returned for reuse. Besides using water that would otherwise go to waste, this system also reduces *greenhouse gas* emissions that would be created with oil or natural gas heating. And the rec center saves more than $70 000 a month on energy bills!

Thermal energy is energy that comes from heat. Tiny particles inside an object generate heat. The faster these particles move, the more heat is created.

What objects have thermal energy? A stove, lightning, a campfire, even your insides!

SUPPLY & DEMAND: WATER

Demand: What We Want	Supply: How We Get It	Big + Small Waste Solutions for Now + the Future
Water for life	Via surface and groundwater. Only 6% of groundwater is replenished every 50 years. What happens if we run out?	Conserve water whenever possible. Example: turning off the tap while you brush your teeth can save 6 L (1.6 gal.) every time.
New water sources	Desalinating ocean water	This could be a great innovation for communities that don't have enough water. But for areas with a plentiful supply, water conservation should be the number-one priority.
New things	Manufacturing requires lots of water and releases harmful chemicals.	Can we learn to live with less stuff?

FOOD

Checking the backpack again. Are you buying lunch or did you pack something? Let's see — a cheese sandwich, an apple, some carrots and two cookies. Where did it all come from — besides the fridge, that is?

Where Did Your Lunch Come From?

Your lunch probably came from all over the world. Many communities rely on other countries to supply their fruits and vegetables. For example, 81 percent of all fruits and vegetables Canadians buy are *imported* from another country. Some are imported because their growing season is limited. Others, such as tropical fruits, don't typically grow in northern climates.

Bread
In the United States, wheat is grown in 42 states. In Canada, wheat is grown in 3 provinces. The wheat travels by rail or barge to bread producers. Then the bread is shipped by truck to stores across the continent.

Cheese
Processed cheese slices are made from cow's milk in North America. Germany, France and the Netherlands are the biggest *exporters* of other cheeses.

Apple
Your apple may come from Washington State or Ontario or any region that has the right growing conditions. Once an apple is picked, it goes to a huge, temperature-controlled storage room, where it waits to be shipped.

Carrots
The United States is fourth on the list of carrot exporters (after China, Uzbekistan and Russia), but if you live in North America, the carrots in your lunch probably come from California or Ontario.

Chocolate-chip cookies
Where did those chocolate chips begin? Many major chocolate brands get their cocoa beans from the Ivory Coast and Ghana.

Eat Locally!

Eating locally means buying food that is produced near the consumer. (That's you, when you buy something.) There is no set distance for what *local* means, but some people use 160 km (100 mi.) as a rule, or within their province or state.

We used to grow our own food or shop close to home because that's what transportation (our walking feet!) allowed. Today, most of us go to supermarkets to get food from all over the world.

The typical lunch travels 2400 km (1500 mi.) from farm to lunch bag.

Depending on where you live, these are some average distances for supermarket foods:

Apples = 2500 km (1553 mi.)
Tomatoes = 2200 km (1367 mi.)
Grapes = 3450 km (2144 mi.)
Lettuce = 3307 km (2055 mi.)

When you eat locally, your food travels a shorter distance. Less transportation means less fuel used, fewer greenhouse gases produced — and less waste!

Eat Sustainably!

If you're eating locally, you're eating sustainably, right? Not necessarily. *Sustainable* comes from the word *sustain*, meaning "keep going" or "support." The ways in which we produce and consume food can help protect and support our environment.

When food is produced in a sustainable way, we:
- protect land and water use
- care for the welfare of animals
- create a safer workplace for farmers and workers
- support local workers
- produce less waste

Food sleuth

Want to find out how your food was made?
At the supermarket checkout, look for the codes.
- If there are four digits and the first one is a 3 or 4, that food was grown conventionally, using science and technology (like fertilizers).
- If there are five digits and the first one is a 9, that food is organic, which means grown without chemical fertilizers or pesticides.
- If there are five digits and the first one is an 8, it was genetically modified (GM). GM organisms are created by taking genes from one species and putting them into another. There are concerns about the harm they may cause.

Banana

Organic Banana

GM Banana

What Is the Foodprint of Your Lunch?

The term *water footprint* is used to describe the amount of water used to make and use or consume something. The *carbon footprint* means the amount of greenhouse gases emitted to produce and use something.

If we combine these footprints, we can picture the *foodprint* of our lunch. A smaller foodprint means less waste!

Water Footprint

For food, the water footprint measures how much water is used to plant, irrigate, package and refrigerate an item.

For example, the water footprint of one vegetarian pizza varies by country because of the availability and quality of water and laws controlling its use.

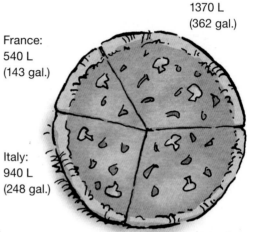

China:
1370 L
(362 gal.)

France:
540 L
(143 gal.)

Italy:
940 L
(248 gal.)

United States:
1200 L
(317 gal.)

Carbon Footprint

A *greenhouse gas* is a gas that absorbs radiation and traps heat in our atmosphere. Greenhouse gases are waste products of certain processes, such as burning oil and gas and other *fossil fuels*. Food production creates greenhouse gases in many ways:

Greenhouse gas	Created by ...
Carbon dioxide (CO_2)	Growing, processing, transporting, storing, cooking and wasting food
Methane (CH_4)	Food waste dumped in landfills; gas from cows
Nitrous oxide (N_2O)	Fertilizers
Sulfur hexafluoride (SF_6)	Electrical equipment
Hydrofluorocarbons (HFCs)	Refrigeration
Perfluorocarbons (PFCs)	Fast-food paper coating

Abbreviations like CO_2 tell us what *chemical elements* make up the gas.

We use CO_2e, which stands for carbon dioxide equivalent, to measure carbon footprints. Some greenhouse gases are more damaging than others, but the CO_2e is an average. It represents all the potential greenhouse gases emitted over a hundred years to produce and use something, added up to a single number.

Up to 17 percent of greenhouse gas emissions from food come from transportation. The rest come from production.

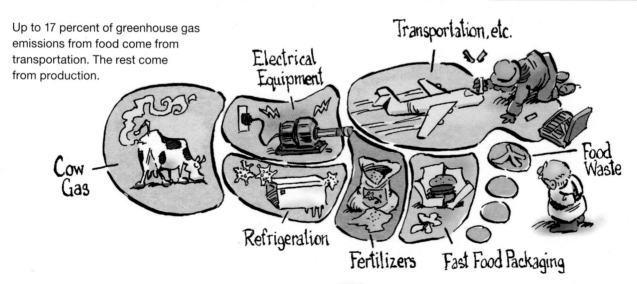

Cow Gas

Electrical Equipment

Transportation, etc.

Refrigeration

Fertilizers

Fast Food Packaging

Food Waste

What's the deal with greenhouse gases and global warming?

The trapped heat leads to *global warming*, which means Earth's temperature is rising.

- When it's hotter, the atmosphere holds on to more moisture. Depending on where you live, this could mean more severe storms or more droughts.
- Warmer weather is melting the polar ice caps, which could cause coastal flooding.
- Droughts can mean less fresh food is grown.

Figuring out your foodprint

Do you carrot all about your lunch waste? (Is that cheesy?) Let's examine some footprints.

Cheese sandwich

How much water went into making this sandwich? For two slices of bread and a slice of cheese:

- Water footprint: 358 L (95 gal.) water

If half of that sandwich goes in the trash, it's like pouring 179 L (47 gal.) of water down the drain. Or flushing a toilet 23 times.

What about the CO_2e emitted to make the sandwich?

- Carbon footprint: 1.4 kg (3 lb.) CO_2e

Or a hamburger?

Beef requires 28 times more land, 11 times more water and creates 5 times more CO_2e than chicken and pork — and way more than cheese. And don't forget the toasted bun.

- Water footprint: 1900 L (500 gal.)
- CO_2e: 8.25 kg (18 lb.)

Apple

- Water footprint: 125 L (33 gal.) — almost a bathtub full
- CO_2e: 170 g (³⁄₈ lb.)

Carrots

- Water footprint: 6.15 L (1⁵⁄₈ gal.)
- CO_2e: 6.8 g (¼ oz.)

Cookies

- Water footprint: 333 L (88 gal.)
- CO_2e: 38 g (1⅓ oz.)

Carton of milk

- Water footprint: 255 L (67 gal.)
- CO_2e: 862 g (2 lb.)

Juice box

- Water footprint: 230 L (61 gal.)
- CO_2e: 898 g (2 lb.)

Look around your classroom and imagine the foodprints of all your classmates. Maybe you have a bigger impact on the planet than you thought!

Want a lunch with less waste? Find out the water and carbon footprints of different foods, so you can make informed decisions. And choose food you know you will eat, so you don't end up throwing it away.

The Food Life Cycle

The life cycle of food shows that waste happens at every stage.

Production
- Bad weather can mean food doesn't grow or ripen properly.
- If a surplus is grown, there's not always enough storage.
- Pests and diseases can spoil the crops.

Processing
- Food is trimmed (like carrot tops) and trimmings are trashed.
- Contamination from bacteria makes waste.

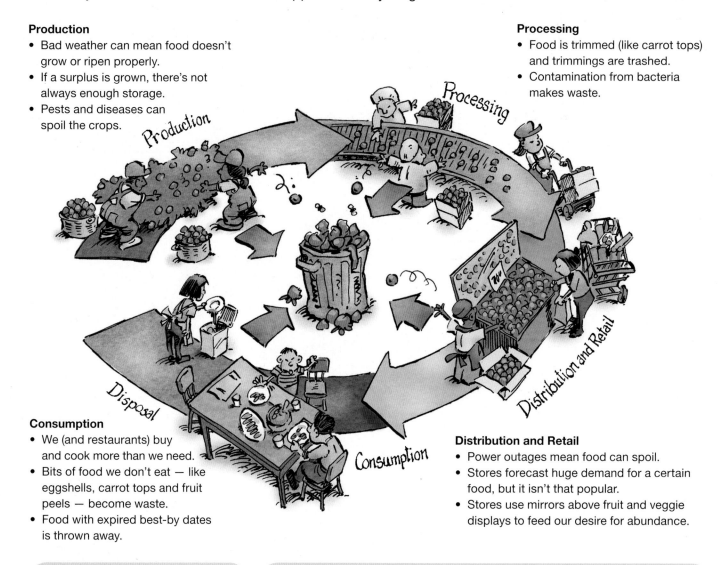

Consumption
- We (and restaurants) buy and cook more than we need.
- Bits of food we don't eat — like eggshells, carrot tops and fruit peels — become waste.
- Food with expired best-by dates is thrown away.

Distribution and Retail
- Power outages mean food can spoil.
- Stores forecast huge demand for a certain food, but it isn't that popular.
- Stores use mirrors above fruit and veggie displays to feed our desire for abundance.

Too ugly?

Supermarkets reject more than 30 percent of fruits and vegetables because *they're too ugly*. Imagine the lowly crooked carrot: "Um, hello? I know I'm not perfect, but check out my gorgeous curves!"

When do we waste the most food?

In developed countries, advanced agricultural technology means food is abundant and cheap. More food is bought — and wasted — at the consumption stage of the food life cycle.

In poorer, developing countries, limited technology and transportation mean that food cannot be harvested and stored in the same way. Refrigeration does not exist in many rural areas. Food waste happens mostly at the production stage.

Each year, more than one-third of the food we produce on Earth is wasted. This equals:
- 1.3 billion tons* of food waste
- $1 trillion
- 3.3 billion tons of carbon dioxide emitted

Do you know what you could buy with $1 trillion? How about *every professional sports league*? Or 167 trips to Mars.

*In this book, 1 ton equals 2000 lb. (a metric tonne equals 1000 kg).

Where Does Food Waste Go?

Landfill-bound food waste

Imagine all the trash cans on your street on garbage day. Almost 40 percent of the waste that goes to a landfill is food.

In the landfill, food waste generates *methane*, one of the greenhouse gases. Food waste creates 17 percent of all global methane (CH_4) emissions. And 300 million barrels of oil are used every year just to make food that ends up in landfills.

Composter-bound food waste

Food for *composting* goes to one of two places — a home composter or a community compost processing plant.

Some home gardeners use backyard composters. Food scraps are added to a closed container that traps heat. The contents are stirred up occasionally. The heat helps decompose the waste, turning leftovers into compost that can enrich garden soil without chemical fertilizers.

In some communities, food waste is collected separately

on garbage day. Large-scale composting is known as *anaerobic* digestion. This process breaks down organic material in an oxygen-deprived container.

These containers are heated to 70°C (158°F) to kill any *microbes*. The composted waste is then rotated for 12 to 14 weeks to aerate the mixture.

The compost is used in public parks and community gardens and shared with local farmers and gardeners. Sometimes composted food waste is used to grow more food!

Digest this!

Greenhouse gases from landfill = bad
The gas created in a landfill comes from compressed layers of food waste and other garbage. A landfill is oxygen-deprived because the weight of the garbage prevents oxygen from getting in. The gas builds up and is released into the atmosphere.

Greenhouse gases from digester = good?
The gas created in a digester, however, is captured. Food waste is "digested," breaking down the sugars, fats, acids and gases and converting them to CH_4 and CO_2. This new mixture does not escape into the atmosphere. Instead, it becomes *biogas*, and it can be used to create heat and electricity. The leftover *effluent* (organic food sewage) can be used for fertilizer and animal feed.

Zoo Poo + Food Waste = Energy?

One of the wonders of food waste is its power to make community and environmental changes. Recovering wasted food and using the excess as fuel — or more food — can make a big difference.

What do you get when you mix zoo poo and food waste? Electricity. Fertilizer. And more food!

It's no joke! This combo is happening right now. The Toronto Zoo will be the first zoo in North America with its own biogas plant.

The biogas plant is being built across the street from the zoo. Animal manure will be brought over and mixed with food waste from local supermarkets in a biogas tank. The fuel will create renewable power for Ontario's electricity grid. This process will reduce greenhouse gas emissions by 10 000 tons of CO_2 per year.

The Zoo Share biogas will also create high-quality fertilizer to go back into the soil, to grow more food.

Biogas Tank

A fresh idea for stale food

Carol Lin, a researcher at the City University of Hong Kong, is turning food waste into something new.

She collects stale baked goods from local bakeries and mixes them with fungi. These break down the baked goods into simple sugars. The sugars are put in biogas tanks (like the one that converts zoo poo), and the bacteria turn the sugar into succinic acid.

This acid is useful in a bunch of products, but researchers are most excited about how it can be used to make biodegradable plastic (*bioplastic*). Other bioplastics are made from crops like corn that still require lots of fertilizers, pesticides and water. Reclaiming food waste to create succinic acid for plastic means using up waste and not creating more.

That stale muffin might help create the container that holds your breakfast tomorrow!

Sharing the harvest

Although food waste is a big problem, 795 million people around the world still do not have enough to eat. That equals about one out of every nine people.

We already have enough food to feed everyone on Earth — if only we could cut the waste and distribute food fairly. Here's how one man is showing the way.

In 1989, Robert Egger began using his refrigerated van to take leftover food from banquets to homeless shelters in Washington, DC. Now his nonprofit organization collects donated food from supermarkets and restaurants and uses it in a program that teaches people who are homeless, unemployed or recently released from prison how to cook. More than 1400 people have found jobs thanks to this training.

Local farmers also give them approximately 362 875 kg (800 000 lb.) of imperfect fruits and vegetables every year to help support the program. The food they collect gets turned into 6300 healthy meals a day for schoolchildren. From leftovers to community change — food waste has power.

SUPPLY & DEMAND: FOOD

Demand: What We Want	Supply: How We Get It	Big + Small Waste Solutions for Now + the Future
The freshest food	From farms, gardens and markets	Buy only what we need. Share it. Follow the FIFO rule for the fridge: "First in, first out!"
Fresh food	By reading the best-before dates on packaging	That food may still be good. Most best-before dates are about freshness, not safety. The only foods legally required to have expiration dates are baby formula and other liquid and medical diets.
All ingredients year-round	From food traveling around the world	Choose (imperfect) summer fruits in summer, winter vegetables in winter.

CLOTHING

Umm ... **How long have those dirty gym clothes been in your backpack? You probably have favorite clothes that you wear over and over again, but unless they are going to a clothing museum, much will end up as clothing waste. Every person in North America throws out an estimated 32 kg (70 lb.) of clothing per year. But let's start at the beginning — what are your clothes made of?**

Cotton

Your T-shirt is likely made from cotton. Twenty million tons of cotton are produced every year.

Recipe for cotton

1 Plant cottonseeds.

2 These sprout flowers. When the flower falls off, a little cup is left.

3 When the cup bursts open, cotton fibers appear and dry in the sun — it's harvest time.

5 Send the cotton to textile mills, where it is spun into thread that is woven into fabric. One bale of cotton weighs close to 230 kg (500 lb.).

4 Pack the cotton into bales and send them to the cotton gin, where fibers are separated from the plant.

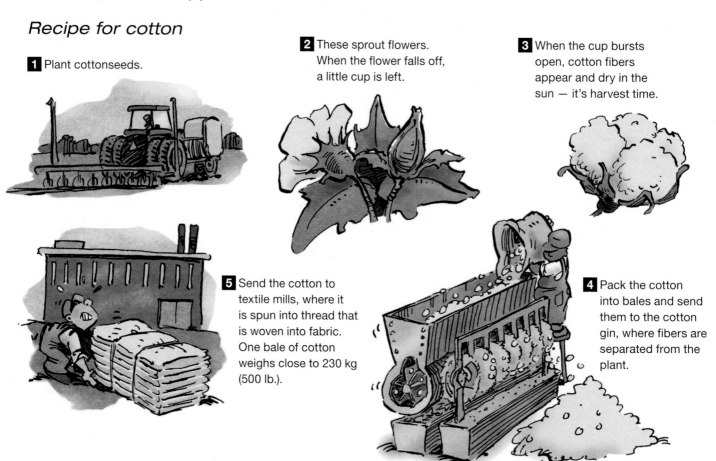

It seems like a totally natural process, right? But cotton is a "thirsty crop" because it requires so much water and creates so much wastewater. It also uses massive amounts of insecticides, herbicides (weed killers) and fertilizers.

To make a T-shirt and jeans:
- 378 g (⅚ lb.) chemicals (insecticides, herbicides and fertilizers)
- 20 000 L (5283 gal.) water

Yield: One bale of cotton can make more than 1200 T-shirts.

Leftovers: Chemicals left over from cotton farming contaminate groundwater and surface water. They also destroy fish and bird populations.

Wool

Do you wear a wool toque in the winter? Almost 1 billion kg (2.2 billion lb.) of wool are produced each year from sheep.

In New Zealand, 90 percent of greenhouse gas emissions are caused by methane from sheep. In scientific circles this is known as the sheep's *enteric fermentation*. Also known as burping and tooting.

Synthetics

Synthetic means made by chemicals, often to imitate a natural product. Chemicals sound suspect, but many are not evil! Some synthetic fabrics are very helpful, like the outer layer of a firefighter's suit.

Synthetics are often used in athletic wear, like your gym shorts, because they are lightweight and dry quickly.

There are hundreds of different synthetic fabrics. Polyester is the most popular.

Polyester
To make polyester, you need a *polymer*, which is a large molecule of repeating units. (DNA is a natural polymer. It is a long chain of protein molecules that makes you who you are.)

Ethylene from crude oil is the main ingredient in polyester. Ethylene (a polymer) is heated together with dimethyl terephthalate (an ester) to create an alcohol. The alcohol and acid are then vacuumed together at very high temperatures.

The resulting clear polyester compound is forced through slots to make long ribbons. The cooled ribbons are cut into chips and then spun into fibers.

Each year 70 million barrels of oil are used to make new polyester clothing.

Yield: Close to 40 million tons of polyester are made every year, about 65 percent for clothing.

Leftovers: Every time a synthetic fabric goes through the wash, it sheds approximately 1900 plastic fibers. Since washers and sewage systems don't have filters to capture the fibers, they end up in the ocean. These fibers add to the 5.25 *trillion* pieces of plastic found in the ocean today.

The T-Shirt Adventure

Take a look at the tag inside your dirty T-shirt. It probably says "Made in So-and-So Country." That means your T-shirt was *assembled* in that country, but parts could have been made in many other countries. How far do you think your T-shirt traveled to make it to your backpack?

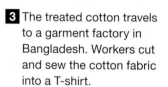

1 Let's start in Texas, the biggest cotton-producing state in America.

2 From there, the cotton fiber may be sent to a mill in China, where it is washed, bleached, dyed and spun into yarn or woven into sheets.

3 The treated cotton travels to a garment factory in Bangladesh. Workers cut and sew the cotton fabric into a T-shirt.

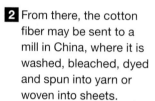

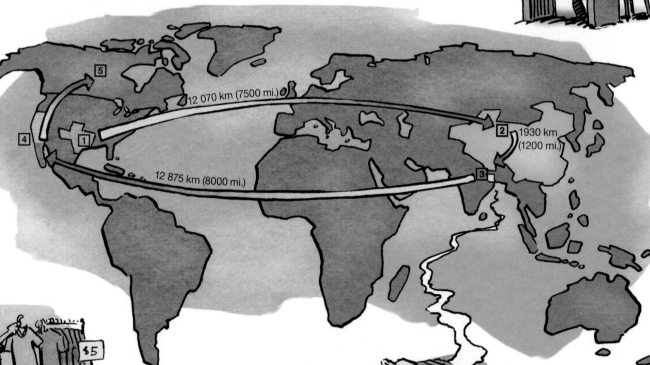

12 070 km (7500 mi.)

1930 km (1200 mi.)

12 875 km (8000 mi.)

5 From there, retailers transport them to their stores or warehouses. How far is it from California to your home? Add on some more travel.

4 The T-shirt returns to North America, to a clothing distribution center. (The largest one is in California.)

Total distance your T-shirt traveled: at least 26 875 km (16 700 mi.)

Clothing Waste

What happens when we're done with our clothing?

It gets donated

Almost 70 percent of donated clothing ends up being sent to Africa. Some is sold in markets there, but much of it gets dumped in local landfills.

Donated clothing is also sold to textile recyclers for cleaning cloths, carpet padding, insulation and furniture stuffing.

It finds love again

As many as 25 percent of North Americans shop at clothing resale shops. This saves 1.1 billion kg (2.5 billion lb.) of clothing waste from the landfill.

It gets trashed

Approximately 85 percent of clothing ends up in a landfill. We buy more clothes now because they are cheaper than they were 20 years ago.

Fast Fashion versus Slow Decomposition

Fast fashion means manufacturers cash in on the latest trends by creating new clothes quickly and cheaply. This often means paying workers less and having them work in unsafe conditions.

At the opposite end of fast fashion is *slow decomposition*. In the landfill, as clothing decomposes, it releases methane, dyes and other chemicals. How slow is decomposition?

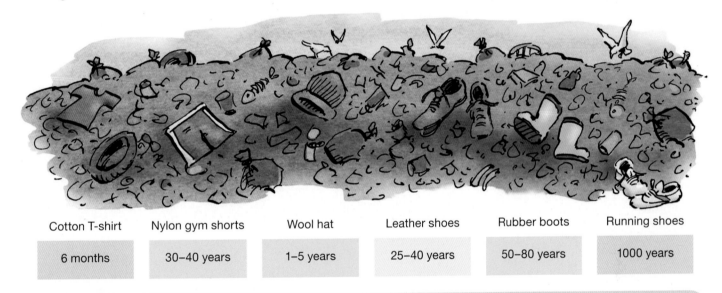

Cotton T-shirt	Nylon gym shorts	Wool hat	Leather shoes	Rubber boots	Running shoes
6 months	30–40 years	1–5 years	25–40 years	50–80 years	1000 years

Why do running shoes take so long to decompose?

Because they have so many parts! The three layers of the sole are made of ethylene vinyl acetate, polyurethane and carbon rubber. The covering is made from fabric like artificial suede or nylon. Usually the laces are cloth and the lace holes are plastic. Industrial glue is used to stick all the parts together.

Communities are finding ways to reuse parts of running shoes for new purposes. For example, some of the materials can be used for playground surfaces. Your shoes can be recycled into a surface for a running track!

How do scientists test for decomposition?
Do scientists sit in a landfill for 40 years watching your gym shorts decompose? Let's hope not!

They use a test called *respirometry*. They place a waste sample into a container with soil and air. The combination allows microorganisms to feast on the sample, which produces CO_2. Then, to determine decomposition, they measure the amount of CO_2 released.

Grow Your Own Fabric

How can we be fashion forward and "green"? Today resourceful designers are experimenting with new and creative ideas for making clothing. How about growing your own fabric from bacteria? Designer Suzanne Lee in England uses this process to grow fabric from kombucha culture bacteria.

1 Brew a large vat of tea.

2 Stir in sugar until it's dissolved.

3 Once it's cool, add in the bacteria and an acid (such as vinegar).

4 After a few days, bubbles start to form. That is a sign that fermentation is happening. The *cellulose* fiber is growing.

6 Dye the fabric using fruit and vegetable stains. After that, it is ready to sew!

5 A few weeks later, the cellulose layer thickens and is ready for harvest. Take the new fabric out of the water and dry it flat.

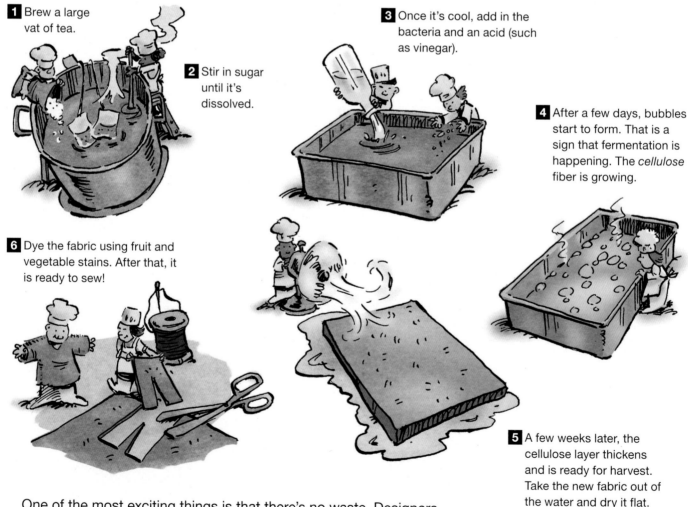

One of the most exciting things is that there's no waste. Designers can grow exactly as much fabric as they need.

As well, it's completely sustainable. Once you're done wearing it, you can simply compost it.

Recycled Plastic Clothing

Instead of using resources to extract oil and create new plastic for polyester, lots of designers are using plastic water bottles as their raw material.

Disposable bottles are washed and cut into plastic flakes. Like "new" polyester, reclaimed plastic is pushed through tiny holes to make strands, then cut, stretched and sent to fabric manufacturers.

How many recycled bottles to make a … ?

T-shirt	🍶	x 14
Backpack	🍶	x 40
Jeans	🍶	x 8
Baseball cap	🍶	x 2

The U.S. women's soccer team has new uniforms — well, kind of new. Every piece — the jersey, shorts and socks — is made from plastic bottles recycled into polyester yarn. Each uniform uses about 18 recycled bottles.

The uniforms are now lighter, which increases players' speed and comfort. But they will still release plastic fibers when washed. Reducing plastic is key!

Surfer clothes from ocean waste

Few people keep a closer eye on the ocean than surfers.

About 640 000 tons of fishing nets get tossed in the ocean every year. What if ocean waste and textile waste could be tackled at the same time?

With a group of others, professional surfer Kelly Slater created a fabric that's a mix of recycled fishing nets, carpets and other nylon waste. This blended fabric is now used to create innovative surfer wear.

Talk about riding the recycling wave!

SUPPLY & DEMAND: CLOTHING

Demand: What We Want	Supply: How We Get It	Big + Small Waste Solutions for Now + the Future
Lots of trendy clothes	Fast, cheap fashion. But this means someone is cutting corners and workers may not be getting a fair wage.	Consider the pre- and post-consumer questions before buying. And buy less!
Typical fabrics	Crops that demand a lot of water, insecticides and herbicides	Clothes made of sustainably grown cotton, hemp and bamboo require fewer (or no) insecticides and herbicides, and create less water waste. Check out the Better Cotton Initiative, which works with everyone in the supply chain to make cotton that is better for the environment.
Bright fabric colors	About 2 trillion L (½ trillion gal.) of water are used every year for dyeing fabrics.	A new technology uses mechanical force instead of water and chemicals to penetrate dye deep into the fabric.

Recycling: Follow the Paper Trail

Do you have a recycling bin in your classroom? Do you put all your waste paper in it, or does some end up in the garbage?

What happens to paper that goes in the recycling bin?

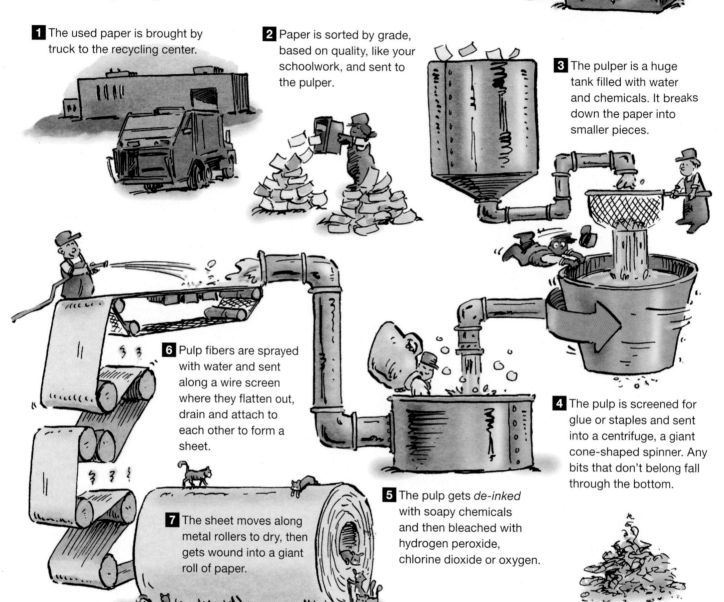

1 The used paper is brought by truck to the recycling center.

2 Paper is sorted by grade, based on quality, like your schoolwork, and sent to the pulper.

3 The pulper is a huge tank filled with water and chemicals. It breaks down the paper into smaller pieces.

4 The pulp is screened for glue or staples and sent into a centrifuge, a giant cone-shaped spinner. Any bits that don't belong fall through the bottom.

5 The pulp gets *de-inked* with soapy chemicals and then bleached with hydrogen peroxide, chlorine dioxide or oxygen.

6 Pulp fibers are sprayed with water and sent along a wire screen where they flatten out, drain and attach to each other to form a sheet.

7 The sheet moves along metal rollers to dry, then gets wound into a giant roll of paper.

How giant is a giant roll of paper? A roll can weigh 18 145 kg (40 000 lb.) — the weight of 4000 cats.

Think Before You Use

You may think that recycling paper makes it okay to throw it out. "It'll be recycled anyway."

It's true that recycling means less logging, deforestation, processing and pulping waste.

But the recycling process has its own demands:

- To make one ton of new office paper = 90 850 L (24 000 gal.) of water

- To make one ton of recycled paper = 45 425 L (12 000 gal.) of water

That's half the water, but still a lot! And recycling paper requires bleaching and de-inking chemicals, as well as lots of energy.

The three *R*s work best when they work together — recycling, reducing and reusing.

Paper Can Be / Can't Be Recycled

Even though we can recycle a lot of it, paper still represents about 30 percent of landfill garbage. In North America, 1.8 million kg (4 million lb.) of wrapping paper goes straight to a landfill every year. That is almost enough paper to cover 6000 professional football fields!

Recyclable	Not recyclable
Office paper, newspaper, magazines, catalogs, junk mail, tissue boxes, the rolls for paper towels and toilet paper, cereal boxes, paper milk and juice cartons, books, paper cups, pizza boxes, cardboard, brown paper bags and shoeboxes	Paper napkins, tissue paper and paper towels (but these can be composted), wax paper, cardboard lined with bubble wrap, waxed cardboard (like from frozen foods) and paper with plastic, metallic or other coatings

Lucky 7

If you see the term "seventh generation," it refers to the Great Law of the Iroquois, which says that we must consider how our decisions will affect the next seven generations. What you buy and use now can have an impact on your great-grandchildren.

Interestingly, seven is also the maximum number of times that paper can be recycled.

Doing Your Bit, Bit by Bit

- Let's say you have a whole piece of paper plus a paper scrap. Which one do you recycle? Both! But most of us don't. Researchers have done experiments and found that whole pieces of paper get recycled and scraps usually get trashed. Why? We tend to only recycle things that still look useful. But even shredded paper can be recycled. Or turned into kitty litter!

- Which is a bigger waster of water — paper napkins or cloth? A paper napkin used once and then thrown away = 15 L (4 gal.) of water. A cloth napkin washed and reused 50 times = 4.5 L (1.2 gal.) of water.
- Recycling paper saves 3855 kg (8500 lb.) of CO_2e per year.

A Recycled-Paper House

When you think of recycled paper, what do you picture? How about a house?

Papercrete is a construction material made primarily from recycled paper. Newspapers, junk mail, magazines and books are mixed with a small amount of clay or cement. The mixture is poured into molds and dried in the sun, then covered with a water-resistant coating. These papercrete bricks are incredibly strong and can be held together with — you guessed it — more papercrete.

Imagine a library made entirely out of recycled books. You could even build your own — but please don't use this book before reading it!

A Recycled-Paper Bike ... and Helmet

Izhar Gafni is an industrial machine designer who created a bike made completely from recycled cardboard and car tires. It weighs less than 9 kg (20 lb.), but can carry up to 125 kg (275 lb.) because of its strong design.

What does every recyclist need? A recycled-paper helmet! Students at the Royal College of Art in London saw all the newspapers left on the subway and wanted to put them to good use. The result: a recycled-paper helmet so light that it's great for people using a bike-sharing program who don't want to lug a heavy helmet around all day.

Wait! What if you leave your paper house to deliver the newspaper on a paper bicycle while wearing a paper helmet? It's possible ...

A Recycled-Paper Canoe

Sure, a cardboard bicycle sounds possible, but a boat? Boats have to get wet!

At the Recycled Cardboard Boat Regatta in Delaware, participants must build their own boat entirely of recycled cardboard — no metal, wood or screws allowed — and paddle it 220 m (720 ft.). Awards are given for Best Decorated Boat, Best Constructed Boat and even Most Dramatic Sinking.

Someday, boats made of recycled paper may actually be practical as well as fun!

The true adventures of comic book paper

1934: The first full-color comic book is printed on groundwood paper — the same paper used for newspapers. The good news: groundwood paper, made by mechanically grinding wood pulp, takes fewer trees and chemicals to produce.

Early 1990s: Popular comics begin printing on 100 percent recycled paper and using soy-based inks rather than traditional petroleum inks. *Hooray!*

Late 1990s: Comics return to paper made from wood because they say recycled paper is too expensive. *Yikes!*

2008: Some comics switch to recycled newsprint paper stock, made from 85 percent paper waste. *Ka-pow!*

Today: The kind of paper comic books use may change again, depending on costs and customer demands. *To be continued ...*

That Quiz Belongs You Know Where ...

Maybe next time you get a quiz back and your results stink, you can do something about it! The White Goat machine is a small paper recycling center with just one purpose. First, you push the waste paper through the shredder. There, the paper dissolves in water. Then it is thinned out and dried, and wound around toilet paper rolls. It takes around 30 minutes to make a roll of TP.

SUPPLY & DEMAND: PAPER

Demand: What We Want	Supply: How We Get It	Big + Small Waste Solutions for Now + the Future
Comics!	New from the store	Instead of throwing away old comics, donate them to soldiers stationed abroad and children in hospitals everywhere.
More recycled paper	Look for post-consumer recycled paper. Right now, about 53% of our paper comes from recycled paper.	By 2020, we will be using 70% recycled paper to make the 500 million tons of paper used around the world.
Mailbox advertisements	The average person receives 18 kg (40 lb.) of junk mail per year. Of this, 44% goes straight to the landfill unopened.	Make your home a junk-mail-free zone.

PLASTIC

What's the drill with plastic? Do you have a plastic bottle in your backpack? Is it reusable or one-use only? Disposable plastic bottles used to be everywhere, but now many schools ban them because of the waste. They are recyclable — aren't they?

From Oil to Plastic

To figure out if something is recyclable, it helps to know how it's made. When it comes to plastic, it all starts with oil.

Oil is usually drilled from areas under the ground called reservoirs. To get to it, you drill through rock.

Metal pipes transport the oil up to huge oil carriers. The carriers deliver the oil to the refinery.

At the refinery, oil is distilled and processed into various petroleum products, including the oil used to make polyethylene terephthalate (PET) plastic.

Recipe for a single-use PET plastic bottle

Ingredients

- Ethylene glycol (from oil)
- Terephthalic acid
- A catalyst (a substance that speeds up the chemical reaction)

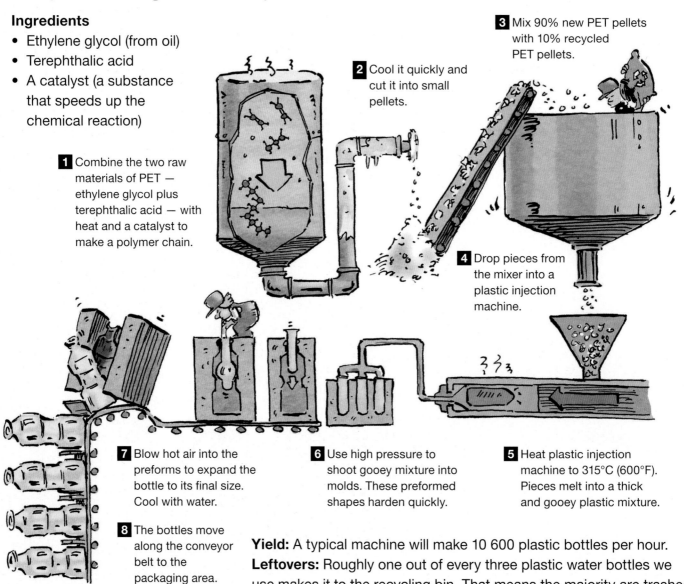

1 Combine the two raw materials of PET — ethylene glycol plus terephthalic acid — with heat and a catalyst to make a polymer chain.

2 Cool it quickly and cut it into small pellets.

3 Mix 90% new PET pellets with 10% recycled PET pellets.

4 Drop pieces from the mixer into a plastic injection machine.

5 Heat plastic injection machine to 315°C (600°F). Pieces melt into a thick and gooey plastic mixture.

6 Use high pressure to shoot gooey mixture into molds. These preformed shapes harden quickly.

7 Blow hot air into the preforms to expand the bottle to its final size. Cool with water.

8 The bottles move along the conveyor belt to the packaging area.

Yield: A typical machine will make 10 600 plastic bottles per hour.

Leftovers: Roughly one out of every three plastic water bottles we use makes it to the recycling bin. That means the majority are trashed.

The top 10 oil-producing countries (per day)

Russia — about 10.5 million barrels

Saudi Arabia — about 9 million barrels

United States — about 9 million barrels

China — about 4.25 million barrels

Iran — about 4 million barrels

Canada — about 3.5 million barrels

Iraq — about 3 million barrels

United Arab Emirates — about 2.95 million barrels

Mexico — about 2.9 million barrels

Kuwait — about 2.75 million barrels

Globally, we produce about 35 billion barrels of oil per year. Only 4 percent is used to make plastic, but that equals about 1.4 million bathtubs full of oil.

SpOILer Alert

Extracting and producing oil has severe environmental consequences from start to finish.

- Drilling begins by carving out roads and clearing trees to deliver massive machinery. Then the ground is broken up, and rock waste is left over.

- One method of extraction is *fracking*. It forces liquid deep underground to cause tiny fractures in rock that contains oil, which allows the oil to flow. This uses lots of water and chemicals. Scientists can't agree on the impact of the fracking process. Some say it is harmless. Others believe it pollutes nearby water sources and can increase the risk of earthquakes.

- Processing oil requires fossil fuel–burning machinery.

- Transporting oil in tankers and along pipelines can lead to leaks, which will poison animals and pollute local water supplies.

- Oil spills create toxic environments for marine life.

33

Plastic versus Glass

Glass bottles began to be mass-produced in the 1800s. New technology and manufacturers' demand for lighter, cheaper and easier-to-make containers spurred the arrival of plastic in 1862.

Which is better, waste-wise? If you're having lunch and a friend pulls out a glass bottle and you have a plastic bottle, which one is better for the environment?

Recipe for glass

We know plastic starts with oil. Glass starts with … sand!

Ingredients

- Silica (SiO_2) from sand
- Sodium carbonate (Na_2CO_3)
- Limestone ($CaCO_3$)
- Cullet (recycled glass)

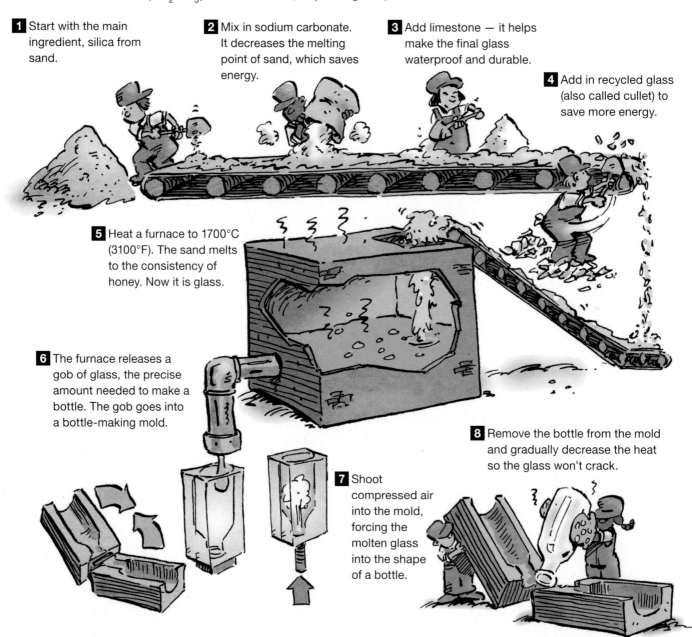

1 Start with the main ingredient, silica from sand.

2 Mix in sodium carbonate. It decreases the melting point of sand, which saves energy.

3 Add limestone — it helps make the final glass waterproof and durable.

4 Add in recycled glass (also called cullet) to save more energy.

5 Heat a furnace to 1700°C (3100°F). The sand melts to the consistency of honey. Now it is glass.

6 The furnace releases a gob of glass, the precise amount needed to make a bottle. The gob goes into a bottle-making mold.

7 Shoot compressed air into the mold, forcing the molten glass into the shape of a bottle.

8 Remove the bottle from the mold and gradually decrease the heat so the glass won't crack.

Yield: Globally, we use almost 50 million tons of glass for containers per year.

Leftovers: The weight of glass makes it expensive to transport. If it breaks en route, most recycling centers send it to the landfill.

The Debate: Single-Use Plastic versus Glass Bottle

Plastic	Glass
Plastic leaches potentially harmful chemicals when heated.	Glass can break — resulting in sharp shards.
Plastic can be recycled and turned into many different things. When recycled, however, it is *downcycled*, which means it becomes a lesser-quality object. There is also a limit to how many times it can be recycled.	Glass can be recycled over and over again without ever losing its quality, but can only become another glass item.
Landfill decomposition time: 500+ years	Landfill decomposition time: 1 million years
30.9% of PET bottles are recycled.	1.3% of glass bottles are recycled.
Total carbon emissions for PET plastic = half the emissions of glass.	Total carbon emissions for glass = twice as much as plastic. (Glass is heavier to transport.)

Verdict: Complicated, right? Use the bottle you intend on wasting the least.

A lunchtime waste audit

Now is a great opportunity for a *waste audit*. A waste audit is an assignment to collect, sort and weigh your overall waste.

Maybe your plastic water bottle gets reused. But not all of them do. Waste studies show that the average kid generates more than 30 kg (65 lb.) of plastic waste from lunch every school year.

Juice boxes are difficult, if not impossible, to recycle because they contain three to six layers of plastic, paper and aluminum that can't be recycled. Scientists estimate that juice boxes will take 350 years to fully break down.

Is this what your lunch table looks like?

Edible spoons

At the end of lunch, does anyone ever say, "No one leaves this table until you've eaten your spoons"? No? Well …

Narayana Peesapaty, a sustainable-farming researcher in the city of Hyderabad, saw everyone on the bus using a plastic spoon. He found out that 120 billion plastic spoons are thrown out in India alone every year.

But what if the spoon became part of the meal? He created different edible spoons made of grains — one for sweet food, another for savory soup or stew. If you don't want to eat it at the end, you can compost it.

Recycling: Plastic by Numbers

Every piece of plastic that was ever made still exists. The pieces of that plastic water bottle from soccer practice two years ago are somewhere on the planet right now ...

The number on the bottom of a plastic item is like a clothing tag — it says a lot about the product.

Plastic #	Examples in your backpack right now ...	Advantages	Disadvantages	We recycle
#1: PETE/PET *Polyethylene terephthalate*		That bottle can be recycled into a tote bag or polar fleece jacket.	Bottle may release chemicals into the liquid	30.9%
#2: HDPE *High-density polyethylene*		Considered one of the safer plastics for food and drink	Trashed HDPE = 200 million pounds of landfill plastic	28%
#3: V *Vinyl or PVC — polyvinyl chloride*		Easy to wipe clean	Considered the most toxic, or poisonous, plastic	0.1–3%
#4: LDPE *Low-density polyethylene*		Good for recycling into playground slides	Put #4 plastic in your recycling bin when it's not recyclable in your area, and the entire haul will be dumped in a landfill.	5.6%
#5: PP *Polypropylene*		Can be recycled into bicycle racks, where you can lock up your paper bike!	Low recycling numbers, even though most curbside service accepts #5	1.7%
#6: PS *Polystyrene*		Recycled polystyrene is being tested as a home insulation material.	Because it is 97% air, it is easily carried by wind and water currents, leading to more ocean waste.	0.8%
#7: Other: a mixed category of both bioplastics and polycarbonates		Is durable enough to protect your noggin	Polycarbonates require high heat and lots of energy to create, and are rarely recycled at the end.	6.1%

PET plastic

PET plastic is a thermoplastic, which means it can soften when heated and harden when cooled to form different shapes for different containers. "Plastic" is from the Greek word *plasticós,* which means "to mold."

What are these bioplastics?

The #7 "other" category includes polycarbonates and bioplastics.

There are three types of bioplastics:

- Bioplastics made from starches like corn, potatoes or rice
- Biodegradable plastics made from petroleum but engineered to break down faster
- "Eco" plastics, made from recycled plastic. Because plastic loses some of its strength with recycling, new bottles cannot contain more than 10 percent recycled material.

Bioplastic pros:

- Some are compostable.
- They require less energy to make.
- They release fewer gases in the landfill.

Bioplastic cons:

- They are not all biodegradable. Some leave a toxic residue after degrading.
- Even bioplastics made from starches use oil in the manufacturing process.
- It still means more plastic in the world!

How much energy is saved by making plastic from recycled plastic instead of making it from oil? About 87 percent!

New life for action figures

Action figures (and fashion dolls) are made of a thermoplastic like PET. Small parts of the figures are made of different plastics like polypropylene and polyethylene. Because of the mixed materials, they are difficult to recycle and usually get tossed in the trash.

Is that any way for an action figure to end its life?

No! Collection centers will accept your old action figures and fashion dolls. They are mechanically separated and molded into new products.

Look out, plastic bags!

Globally, we use 4 billion plastic bags a year. We use them for an average of 12 minutes, but they take 500-plus years to decompose in a landfill. They were first introduced to supermarkets in 1977. So that first bag may be gone by the year ... 2477?

Most plastic bags won't decompose (*biodegrade*) easily because the polymers in them are not recognized as food by microorganisms and they won't eat them.

When 16-year-old Daniel Burd of Waterloo, Ontario, wondered if there was anything he could do to speed up decomposition, he began an experiment.

First, he mixed landfill dirt in with yeast and tap water. Then he added in pieces of the plastic bag. He let it sit for 12 weeks and tested the resulting bacterial culture. The plastic in the solution lost more than 17 percent of its weight!

He isolated the bacteria and started again — this time for six weeks. The bag lost 43 percent of its weight! The bag pieces degraded entirely in three months.

Can future recycling stations include giant bacteria-boosted composters for plastic bags?

Ocean Garbage

What on earth are we throwing into our oceans? It's time to take plastic measures.

In the Clothing chapter, you read that there are 5.25 *trillion* pieces of plastic trash in our oceans. This plastic waste collects in gyres, which are huge, spiraling currents. Rotating currents and powerful winds converge in the area around gyres and carry the pieces around the globe.

The plastic waste doesn't break down completely, but shreds into smaller pieces. Fish and birds mistake rice-sized pieces for food and can die from eating them.

An Ocean Cleanup Innovation

When Boyan Slat was traveling the world, he couldn't believe all the plastic he was seeing in the ocean. After months of research, the 19-year-old designed an ocean cleanup system that collects plastic without harming sea life.

His innovation is a network of anchored floating barriers that work with ocean currents and winds to move the ocean waste to a collection platform. Collected plastic is removed and recycled. The system doesn't use extra energy because it sits and waits for the ocean currents to bring the trash to it. Sea life swims beneath, avoiding being caught. The goal? To remove 7 250 000 tons of ocean waste.

Powered by plastic

Like sewage and food waste, plastic waste contains energy, too. That plastic bottle still has potential as an energy source, thanks to the oil used to make it.

When the plastic bottle goes to a landfill, not only is it contributing to the waste problem, it's a missed opportunity to harness the fuel inside it.

Waste-to-energy facilities convert plastic into fuel. They incinerate the plastic, which creates steam, drives a turbine and creates fuel. The fuel created from burning landfill plastic could be used to generate electricity to power your electronic devices.

Some people believe waste-to-energy incinerators discourage recycling and make more waste. Others argue it is better than just dumping garbage.

Plastic without oil: pig-pee plastic?

Urine luck — a use for all of that pig pee! A chemical company in Denmark wants to use compounds in urine to create the building blocks of plastic.

About 90 000 tons of pig urine are released every day from the billions of pigs around the world. A chemical in the pig's urine called urea can be collected and used as a replacement for petroleum.

Usually, pig pee is dumped into storage tanks that can leak and overflow and pollute the nearby ground and water. Disposing of it is hazardous and expensive.

When used for plastic, though, pig pee can be filtered immediately. The environmental impact and costs are much less than with fossil fuel plastics.

SUPPLY & DEMAND: PLASTIC

Demand: What We Want	Supply: How We Get It	Big + Small Waste Solutions for Now + the Future
A quick drink	Water in a plastic bottle	In most areas, tap water goes through stricter bacteria testing than bottled water. Drink filtered tap water and stop pouring money down the drain!
Single-use items, like spoons or straws	With an on-the-go food or drink	Skip the straw. Or eat the spoon!
Bags to carry our shopping home	Plastic bags are in stores everywhere.	Governments all over the world are banning plastic bags. Bring your own reusable bags!

METALS

Archaeologists love finding metal artifacts, because they can learn a lot about a community by examining how they were made. Is there anything made of metal in your backpack right now?

Aluminum

One metal object you probably see around you all the time is the aluminum drink can. We know aluminum is a metal, but where does it come from?

Recipe for aluminum

Ingredients

- Bauxite (containing aluminum *ore*)
- Sodium hydroxide
- Coal for smelting
- Cryolite

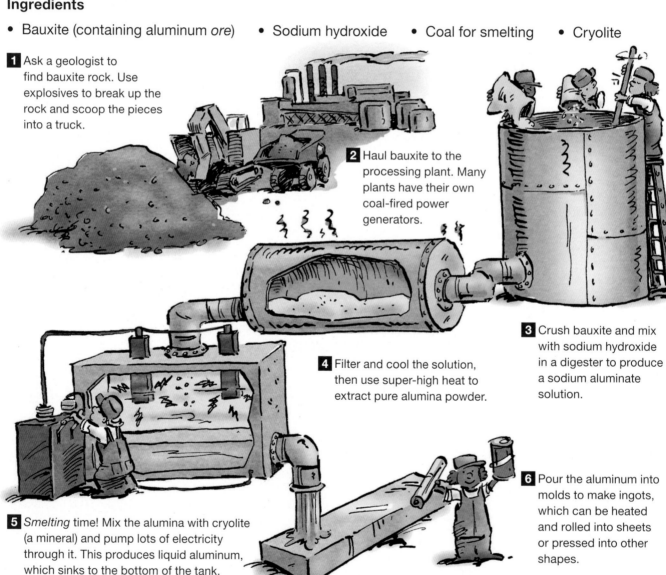

1 Ask a geologist to find bauxite rock. Use explosives to break up the rock and scoop the pieces into a truck.

2 Haul bauxite to the processing plant. Many plants have their own coal-fired power generators.

3 Crush bauxite and mix with sodium hydroxide in a digester to produce a sodium aluminate solution.

4 Filter and cool the solution, then use super-high heat to extract pure alumina powder.

5 *Smelting* time! Mix the alumina with cryolite (a mineral) and pump lots of electricity through it. This produces liquid aluminum, which sinks to the bottom of the tank.

6 Pour the aluminum into molds to make ingots, which can be heated and rolled into sheets or pressed into other shapes.

Yield: Globally, we use about 180 billion aluminum drink cans a year.
Leftovers: Producing 900 kg (1 ton) of aluminum cans creates 4500 kg (5 tons) of corrosive rock waste and releases harmful perfluorocarbons.

Steel and stainless steel

Stainless steel water bottles have become popular alternatives to plastic water bottles.

Also made of stainless steel? The very top of New York City's Chrysler Building. The building itself is made from 29 961 tons of steel.

What's the difference between steel and stainless steel? Their composition.

Steel is made of iron and carbon. It is very strong and used mainly in construction.

The recipe for stainless steel changes depending on what you want to make. The *alloys* you add change the material.

- Iron and chromium stainless steel is used for water bottles and silverware.
- Iron plus chromium plus nickel is used for trains and elevators.

Every year, approximately 27 million tons of stainless steel are made from 16 million tons of recycled steel scraps.

A lot of energy and resources are used to make a stainless steel bottle. But it lasts longer than a plastic bottle, and the alloys can be recovered if you recycle it.

Pump Some Iron!

The main ingredient in steel is iron. How do we get the iron we need?

1 Blast iron-rich taconite rock using explosives.

2 Transport the rocks to a plant. Crush them into pieces, mix with water and grind into a powder.

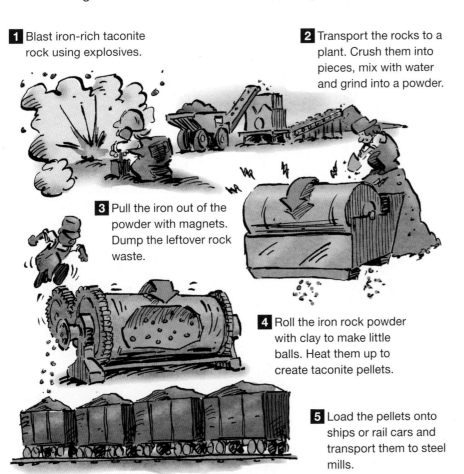

3 Pull the iron out of the powder with magnets. Dump the leftover rock waste.

4 Roll the iron rock powder with clay to make little balls. Heat them up to create taconite pellets.

5 Load the pellets onto ships or rail cars and transport them to steel mills.

What does mining leave behind?

In Minnesota's Iron Range, where iron has been mined for more than 130 years, the rock waste weighs 400 000 tons. That equals 300 football fields stacked 18 m (60 ft.) high.

This leftover rock contains chemicals like cyanide, mercury and arsenic that run through pipes into nearby waterways. This contaminates the water that people and animals depend on for living.

Plus there is all the waste metal. Considering the work that goes into extracting and processing metals, it's too bad how much gets trashed every year. How much? Enough to build 8000 jumbo jets.

Yes, You Can: Recycling Aluminum

Recycling aluminum saves 95 percent of the greenhouse gas emitted to make new aluminum. Here's how that can is recycled:

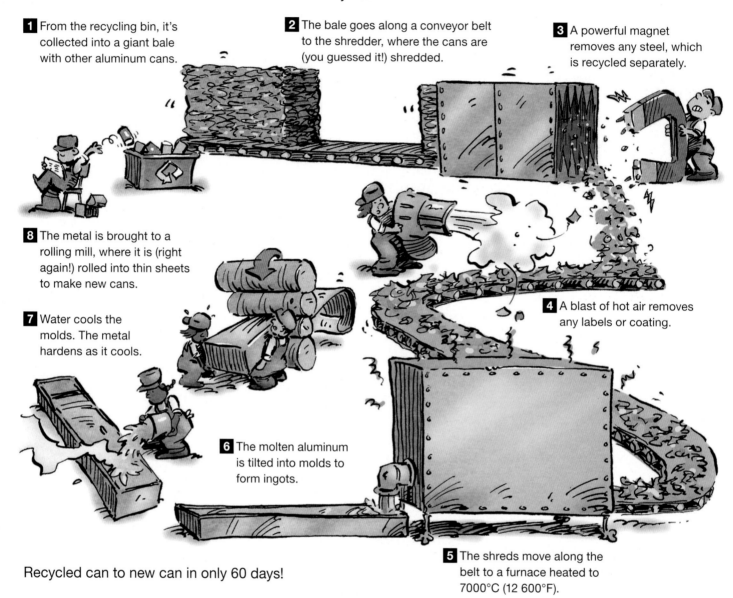

1 From the recycling bin, it's collected into a giant bale with other aluminum cans.

2 The bale goes along a conveyor belt to the shredder, where the cans are (you guessed it!) shredded.

3 A powerful magnet removes any steel, which is recycled separately.

8 The metal is brought to a rolling mill, where it is (right again!) rolled into thin sheets to make new cans.

7 Water cools the molds. The metal hardens as it cools.

4 A blast of hot air removes any labels or coating.

6 The molten aluminum is tilted into molds to form ingots.

5 The shreds move along the belt to a furnace heated to 7000°C (12 600°F).

Recycled can to new can in only 60 days!

Another kick at the can

If aluminum recycling were a school assignment, your teacher might write, "Great start, but you seem to lose your point." That's because in the 1990s, we recycled 60 percent of our cans, and today we recycle only 51 percent.

Why aren't we recycling all of them?

The real energy comes not from the drink inside, but from the can itself.

- Entirely recyclable!
- Less mining! Less smelting!
- Reduce pesky greenhouse gases!
- Recycle forever, without loss of strength!

Uses for Recycled Aluminum

32% = Aluminum siding and other construction materials

28% = Machinery

28% = Transportation (airplanes, cars, boats and trains)

12% = Other (bikes, wiring, etc.)

What's a ferrule?

That metal that holds the eraser on your pencil, usually made of aluminum, is called a ferrule. Most of the 14 billion pencils made every year go to landfills, but now some collection centers recycle them.

Wrap It Up

Your sandwich is wrapped in plastic wrap. Your friend's is wrapped in aluminum foil. Which wrap is better for the environment?

The Debate: Aluminum Foil versus Plastic Wrap

Aluminum foil	Plastic wrap
Producing aluminum requires five to six times less energy than producing plastic.	Producing LDPE plastic releases less CO_2 into the air than producing aluminum.
Foil is not usually accepted in recycling bins because food sticks to it.	The chemicals that make plastic wrap sticky cannot be recycled with other plastic films.
Foil does not biodegrade.	In the landfills, without exposure to light, plastic wrap may never biodegrade.
Foil can be washed and reused over and over.	Plastic can be used only once.

Verdict: Tricky, right? Best to be safe and use a reusable container.

What to do when the chips are done

It's time for a waste challenge:
1. Next time you have chips in a foil bag, keep the empty bag.
2. Crumple it up and then let go.
3. Did it pop back to its original shape?
   (a) If it did, it can't be recycled because the metal and plastic are melded together. Put it in the garbage.
   (b) If it didn't, and stayed crumpled, please recycle it!

Most of the 17 billion chip bags produced each year in the United States end up as landfill.

Why? Because they are made of seven compressed layers of metal and plastic, they can't be recycled because facilities can't separate the materials.

Why are we using materials that we can't recycle? That's a good question. The more companies that use recyclable packaging, the less expensive it will be to make them, and the less waste for our planet.

From Garbage Dump to Orchestra

Some ideas deserve a metal!

Cateura, Paraguay, is a community of 2500 people built around a huge garbage dump. People moved in to make their living as waste pickers.

Favio Chavez, an environmental technician, saw children playing on the mound of trash. He and Don Cola Gomez, a trash worker and carpenter, envisioned another life for the kids and for the trash, too.

Their idea? Turning metal trash into instruments:

- A drum skin made of a silver X-ray plate
- Guitars built with metal dessert tins
- Violins made with aluminum oven trays
- Cellos made of steel oil barrels
- Saxophones and trumpets made from old drainpipes, with keys made from coins

The Recycled Orchestra of Cateura — also known as the "Landfillharmonic" — brings great pleasure to the community, performing concerts at home and worldwide. The beauty that can be created out of garbage is inspiring.

How sweet it is

Candy wrappers usually suffer the same fate as chip bags. Most are made of foil and paper, sometimes with a plastic coating. These last for more than 400 years in a landfill.

Some candy makers are unhappy that their products create so much garbage. Would a 100 percent compostable wrapper be possible?

Yes! Designers have created a wrapper made of wood-pulp-based material and using non-toxic inks. The small amount of aluminum decomposes with the help of bacteria and worms in composters.

Can you convince your favorite candy manufacturer to start using these new wrappers?

Time for another waste challenge!
1. Find a candy maker that uses 100 percent compostable wrappers.
2. Eat the candy.
3. What should you do with the wrapper?
   (a) Compost it.
   (b) Bury it in your garden.
   (c) Burn it in a fireplace or campfire.
   (d) Any of the above

Yes — d is the right answer. Any of these options will disintegrate the wrapper safely.

Tap Into Scrap

Driving a car is not always a great choice for the environment. But *recycling* one?

About 65 percent of a car is made of steel. Steel is the most recycled consumer material.

Recycling steel requires 70 percent less energy than making steel from iron ore. Recycling one car saves:

- 1135 kg (2500 lb.) of iron ore
- 635 kg (1400 lb.) of coal
- 11 700 kg (25 800 lb.) of steel
- 148 000 L (39 000 gal.) of water!

Approximately 14 million tons of steel are recovered from cars every year. The scrap metal is recycled for all kinds of purposes.

- 1 recycled car = 4 steel utility poles
- 1 recycled car = 1300 steel bicycle frames
- 1 recycled car = 175 file cabinets
- 1 recycled car = 1 steel frame for a small house

Other recyclable parts include rubber tires, textiles from seats, glass windows, copper wiring and aluminum parts.

So yes, recycling is a great choice for a car that is going nowhere.

SUPPLY & DEMAND: METALS

Demand: What We Want	Supply: How We Get It	Big + Small Waste Solutions for Now + the Future
To quench that thirst	From a can	Recycle it every time.
A combination lock for your locker	A new one every year	Keep our memories sharp and remember the combination? Less replacement waste.
Snack foods!	From chips and candy bars wrapped in foil combinations	Compostable bags and wrappers in the future? No one is suggesting a life without snacks …

ELECTRONICS

Do you have a cell phone in your backpack? For many, that cell phone is a lifeline. It helps us communicate, take photos and stay up to date. But, like all electronic lifelines, it has an end. What happens when you are done with it? Unless you pass it along to someone else, it will become e-waste.

What Is E-Waste?

E-waste, or electronic waste, is an electronic device that gets trashed or recycled. An electronic device is anything with a battery or electrical cord, not just a screen — so that includes toasters and vacuum cleaners. The biggest sources of e-waste are TVs, computers, monitors, cell phones, DVD players, headphones, game consoles, e-readers and digital cameras. How is that cell phone made? To understand its end, we need to know its beginning.

Recipe for a cell phone

This is our most complicated recipe yet. So many ingredients! A cell phone is made of 40 percent metals, 40 percent plastics and 20 percent ceramics and trace materials.

Ingredients

For the glass screen:

- Aluminum oxide: mined from bauxite (see Metals chapter)
- Silicon dioxide: made from mining quartz
- Indium tin oxide: indium is a soft, silver-white metallic element mined from zinc and tin ores (ore is rock that contains enough minerals to extract the elements inside)
- Rare earth elements like yttrium, lanthanum, terbium, praseodymium, europium, dysprosium and gadolinium, mined from carbonatite and alkaline rocks
- Water, to polish the glass

Rare earth elements are metals with similar properties found together in rock deposits. The unique properties they have in common are magnetism, luminescence and electrochemical power. In other words, they can create a strong electrical charge and emit light.

For the case:
- Aluminum alloys (see Metals chapter)
- Plastic from crude oil (see Plastic chapter)
- Flame retardants are stuck to the circuit board and inside the plastic case. The chemical compound mixes bromide (a toxic chemical element) with bisphenol A, or BPA, a synthetic compound used to make plastic.

For the battery:
- Lithium cobalt oxide: made from lithium carbonate and cobalt, a magnetic metal
- Graphite: a crystalline form of carbon, made artificially and also mined
- Aluminum for the casing

For the wires:
- Gold: used as a conductor of low-voltage currents. Mined from quartz and extracted by breaking down the rock.
- Copper: mined from copper ore
- Silver: a rare element in Earth's crust, but mined from minerals like argentite

For the circuitry:
- Platinum: rare to find on its own, but mined from some nickel and copper ores
- Tungsten: mined from scheelite and wolframite
- Silicon (and water): for the microchips, which contain the circuits

For the microphone:
- Nickel: mined from pentlandite, garnierite and limonite ores

(The next six ingredients are rare earth elements.)

For the speaker magnets:
- Praseodymium
- Gadolinium
- Neodymium

For the vibration unit:
- Neodymium
- Terbium
- Dysprosium

Cell phone ingredients are mined, collected and transported from many countries all over the world.

Assembly and distribution
1. Collect the ingredients and ship to a manufacturing facility. Some components come already assembled.
2. Assemble the many components.
3. Wrap the phone in paper and plastic.
4. Ship it to distribution centers around the globe.

Yield: There are currently 7.3 billion active cell phones in the world.

Leftovers: Every two years, more than 7 billion cell phones are replaced. That equals a dizzying amount of e-waste.

E-Waste Options

The Statue of Liberty in New York weighs 225 tons. We throw out 50 million tons of e-waste each year. That equals more than 222 000 statues! It's time to get charged up about e-waste!

E-waste is tricky, however, because an electronic product can contain 1000 different substances. Some materials are valuable and others are toxic, or poisonous.

Some of the toxic substances include chlorinated solvents, PVC, heavy metals and lead. A cathode ray tube in your old TV or computer monitor can contain around 1.8–3.6 kg (4–8 lb.) of lead.

As for valuable substances, in one million cell phones there are 2390 kg (5269 lb.) of copper, 350 kg (772 lb.) of silver and 34 kg (75 lb.) of gold.

The Good News!

Electronic waste can be recycled safely. With more electronics in the world, companies are figuring out safe ways to recycle and reuse parts.

The best process:

1. Non-toxic materials like steel, aluminum, metals and glass are removed. They are sold to smelters and the raw materials are used again. Plastic pellets go to plastic recyclers.

2. Cables and wires, circuit boards and other electronic parts are separated for metal recovery. They can be sold to metal refiners.

3. Glass and batteries are sent on a conveyor belt to be crushed. A magnet pulls metal out of the mix. The cathode ray tube is removed.

Recycling one million laptops saves the energy equivalent of electricity used by 3500 homes.

The Not-So-Good News ...

A lot of e-waste goes to the landfill or incinerator, or is illegally and unsafely disposed of in developing countries.

E-waste that goes into the landfill or incinerator	E-waste that gets "recycled" in developing countries
About 60% goes to the landfill.	Workers earn low wages in unsafe conditions.
Lead, cadmium and mercury get leached into the ground and groundwater.	Workers (without protective clothing or masks) melt computer circuit boards over a coal fire. Toxic compounds enter the air.
E-waste burned in an incinerator releases lead, mercury and cadmium into the atmosphere.	Acid, which can burn skin, is used to melt other computer and electronic parts.
E-waste makes up 70% of the heavy metals found in solid-waste landfills.	E-plastic is melted and reused for downcycled plastic products that might retain toxic substances.

The Debate: E-reader versus Paper Book

E-reader	Paper book
Mining raw materials for lithium batteries creates erosion and soil contamination.	Paper production emits greenhouse gases.
Uses non-renewable resources like columbite-tantalite (capacitors) and mercury (screens)	The paper industry is responsible for lots of deforestation.
More fossil fuels are used for electricity at data centers.	Does not require a power supply to use (besides your brain)
Electric infrastructure is required to connect and transmit data over distances.	Even using recycled paper, de-inking requires a lot of water and releases chemical waste.
On average, 300 L (79 gal.) of water are used to produce an e-reader.	On average, 26 L (7 gal.) of water are used to produce a book.
Some companies have certified recycling facilities for their e-reader buy-back programs.	Paper books are recyclable.
You can't share e-reader books.	You can share paper books.

Verdict: Like so many issues with waste, it's not always clear. Keep reading, though, because maybe in one of those books you'll discover a great idea for our planet's future.

Cracking down on illegal e-wasters

The Basel Convention is an international treaty enacted in 1989 to stop the illegal trading of e-waste between countries.

Investigators found that 80 percent of the electronics sent for recycling were actually being shipped to developing countries and dismantled with no concern for the health of people or planet. They cracked down on the shady companies that were guilty of this practice.

Consumers can now research the e-waste recycler to confirm that it is Basel Action Network certified.

New Life for Cell Phones

Are electronics designed to fail? Is it possible to make electronics last longer, but tech companies don't want to because it means fewer sales? Is an "upgrade" always essential?

A cell phone with removable, fixable parts

What if the inner components of your phone were easily removable? Owners could update features without having to buy a whole new phone. They could rent, buy or exchange only the parts needed. This would save on money and help keep phones from becoming e-waste.

Industrial designers are working on a new cell phone model that comes in separate parts. The base phone can be connected to separate pieces for batteries, processors, cameras and displays. Consumers would pay only for the features they really want.

Recycled cell phones as rain forest guardians

Deforestation produces more greenhouse gases every year than all of the world's cars, ships, trains and planes combined. Illegal logging in the rain forest is a big part of the deforestation problem.

The Rainforest Connection organization uses old phones to protect the natural world. They take a recycled cell phone, add in solar panels and hide it in the tree canopy. It is programmed with a sensitive microphone that listens for the sounds of chain saws. (Each device can hear within a 1 km [3/5 mi.] distance.) When it hears a sound, it sends a message to a local cloud network. The data is analyzed and a team is sent into the forest to stop the logging on the spot.

Industrial Robots Tackle Waste

Researchers in Australia have developed a robot that can take apart e-waste. These robots memorize the design of electronics and then work backward to disassemble the product. Cognitive robotics gives them the intelligence to respond to complex goals.

A big benefit: robots can safely recycle even the toxic parts. They are not at risk from the chemicals released during the recycling process. Another way robots have us beat? They can work 24/7 without a break.

Be e-smart!

Improperly discarded e-waste can leave people and organizations open to security threats. Phones and computers contain personal information that can be used by people looking for financial statements, credit card numbers and bank accounts.

Wipe your memory clean before you say goodbye to your electronic device!

SUPPLY & DEMAND: ELECTRONICS

Demand: What We Want	Supply: How We Get It	Big + Small Waste Solutions for Now + the Future
Cool electronic devices	By upgrading with new releases	Upgrading means improving to a higher quality. But with all our e-waste, how are we "upgrading" the planet? Can we hold on to our devices for longer?
Cool electronic toys powered by batteries	When we buy new things, the older model hits the trash. Lead-acid and nickel-cadmium batteries contaminate soil and water.	Recycle those batteries! The recycling facility breaks them apart and recycles the plastic and lead for new batteries.
New video games and consoles	The old one goes to a landfill, where phthalates, bromine, PVC and other toxic materials take 1000-plus years to break down.	Donate that old console to charity. Or check the Basel Action Network to see which recyclers are trustworthy. There should be no shame in the game!

WASTE IN SPACE

The contents of your backpack can represent all the things we need here on Earth: water, food, clothing and communication. But what if you had only what's in your backpack to survive? And what if there was no landfill or recycling center? Space travel experts can teach us a lot about living with *zero waste*.

The Ultimate Backpack

The backpack that astronauts use is called the Primary Life Support Subsystem. It manages both life needs and waste.

- *Oxygen ventilation:* a closed-loop system, where oxygen circulates through the backpack and into the space suit, and carbon dioxide is filtered out with a charcoal cartridge
- *Condensation:* perspiration and breathing create a lot of water. This water is pulled from the oxygen and sent to water storage tanks.
- *Feedwater circuit:* pressure from the oxygen moves the water from the storage tanks to two steel plates. As the water evaporates, it helps to cool the plates — and the astronaut's body temperature.
- *Liquid transport circuit:* helps keep the body temperature stable
- *Jet pack:* holds thruster jets for flying back to the space station!

Essential Resource Planning

Modern space programs are examining their needs and waste to create more sustainable missions. Astronauts require a precise amount of water, oxygen and food per day. Their use and waste are carefully calculated when planning space trips.

Daily consumption + waste

Every day on the International Space Station (ISS) …	Every day on Earth …
I generate 3.8 L (1 gal.) of water waste, including washing dishes!	I generate about 287 L (75 gal.) of water waste. Eek!
Each day I consume 7.5 L of oxygen (2 gal.). I exhale 1 L (¼ gal.) of CO_2, which is removed with a chemical process.	I consume 550 L of oxygen (145 gal.). I exhale as much CO_2 as my astronaut friend, but it's removed with the help of green plants!
I eat 0.6 kg (1⅓ lb.) of special space food and from that generate 0.1 kg (⅕ lb.) of solid waste.	I eat about 2 kg (4½ lb.) of food. From that, I create 2 kg (4½ lb.) of solid waste.

Other space travel essentials

Space bathroom

Keeping astronauts hydrated in space used to be a costly undertaking. Water was delivered to the space station via cargo rockets. And wastewater was vented out into space.

That changed in 2003, when a wastewater distillation system was created. The system has filters that transform crew members' urine and sweat into clean drinking water. It creates 2725 kg (6000 lb.) of *potable water* per year.

What about poo in space? Is that a shooting star? No, um …

Instead of hurtling through our solar system at 28 165 km/h (17 500 mph), poo is usually stored until the mission returns to Earth. A new study, though, is examining how it could be used to create fertilizer for growing more space food.

Space food

When you read *space food*, do you think of freeze-dried ice cream and power bars? The ISS has an indoor plant cultivation system for growing fruits and vegetables. This system teaches crew members about growing food in different conditions and how to live more sustainably.

This technology could be helpful for us as we figure out how to feed our growing world population.

A one-year space mission on the ISS produces about 3900 kg (8600 lb.) of food waste. Some of it is used as fertilizer for the plant cultivation system.

Space clothing

Since washing machines aren't an option in space, dirty space clothes are typically bundled and shot into Earth's atmosphere to burn up. A six-person crew can generate 408 kg (900 lb.) of clothing per year.

NASA researchers are looking at synthetic fibers that are lightweight and resist body odor. Astronauts could wear their clothes for longer, even when they exercise.

Imagine what that could mean for gym clothing on Earth! Could *we* use the technology to generate less clothing waste and water usage?

Space Waste

What is space waste? It's nice to think of space as endless black sky between stars and planets.

But there's an awful lot of space waste spinning around our universe.

Space waste is the stuff left over from launches: bits of satellites, rockets and waste from the crew. Even though current space missions treat their waste carefully, there's still a space waste problem.

What do satellites do?

Satellites take pictures of Earth, the moon and our orbit. Some send back information about our atmosphere, weather patterns and oceans. Others are communication satellites, used for phone, TV and radio signals. NASA uses satellites to track the size, speed and altitude of orbiting space waste.

Waste Rules!

In 2007, the United Nations released guidelines for reducing space waste. Could we use these rules, too?

Space waste timeline	
1950s:	Satellites begin launching into space.
1960s:	Satellites are left to drift or burn up upon reentering the atmosphere.
1999:	The ISS performs its first collision-avoidance maneuver and avoids hitting a discarded rocket.
2004:	Part of a global positioning system (GPS) satellite falls and lands in Argentina.
2012:	The moon's surface has something like 181 435 kg (400 000 lb.) of waste on it, including 70 spacecraft, 12 pairs of boots, TV cameras and empty space-food packages.
Today:	Of the fragments in orbit, 20 000 are bigger than a melon. More than 100 million are less than the width of your thumb. A piece this size can cause a crack in a spacecraft's windshield.
The future:	Scientists predict that space waste will triple by 2030. Will that endanger the satellites we rely on?

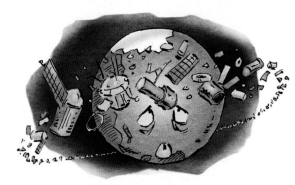

Guidelines for avoiding space waste	Guidelines for avoiding Earth waste
Space systems should be designed not to release space junk during normal operations.	Every design should include a plan for eliminating or reusing waste.
Space systems should be designed to avoid accidental breakups.	Avoid making or purchasing items for single use or that are not designed to last.
Intentionally destroying any spacecraft in space is not allowed.	No littering!
To avoid post-mission explosions, any stored energy should not be left in abandoned spacecraft.	Stored energy within items — like biogas in food or crude oil in plastic — should be used as fuel.
Abandoned spacecraft should be removed in a controlled way.	Leftover e-waste should be taken apart in a controlled way.
Spacecraft that could interfere in the region of outer space near Earth should be left in other orbits.	Waste created in other countries affects all of us because we share this planet.

Space Waste to Worldship?

Perhaps there's a use for some of this space waste? Designers, architects, engineers, scientists and sociologists have been designing a space dwelling called the Worldship.

The Worldship is meant to launch from Earth and stay in space, supporting generations of life inside. Synthetic soil made from space waste will sustain human, plant, animal and microbe life with the help of tiny sensors. The goal is to create interstellar life for humans by the year 2100.

Why don't we launch our own garbage up into space?

Hello, Earthlings!

We know what you think — that if you launch your garbage toward the sun, it will just burn up. But you're wrong. It won't reach the sun and will stay floating in your outer atmosphere. Do you want to look at the night sky and see a garbage trail?

Also, we know how much money you have and you can't afford it. Each pound of trash would cost you more than $11 000. This equals trillions of dollars per day. Do you really want to send your trash on a pricey space adventure?

Let's make a deal — you clean up your mess and we'll clean up ours. Even though we don't make a mess (because we're aliens and superior beings).

ZERO-WASTE FUTURE

From recycled urine to sweat-resistant clothing, space travel can inspire us to think differently about resources. The goal of a closed-loop system is zero waste. No wasted resources, no landfill.

Zero waste is a philosophy that considers each stage of production and use to minimize waste. Products are made to be used, reused, recycled or repaired.

A Zero-Waste Classroom

Simple switches can result in big waste changes:
- Use reusable containers and lunch bags.
- Compost lunch and snack waste.
- No more plastic cutlery or disposable bottles!
- Use 100 percent post-consumer-waste recycled paper, and recycle it when done.
- Use natural light as much as possible.

- Turn off computers when not in use. Ensure they are safely recycled at the end.
- Trash talk with another class — have a zero-waste competition to see who's the greenest!
- Consider when you eat. When kids eat lunch after recess instead of before, they end up throwing out 30 percent less food.

Taiwan, a Zero-Waste Leader

When the island country of Taiwan experienced an industrial boom, that was good for the economy but meant more waste. Here's how Taiwan adopted a zero-waste philosophy:

Pay for packaging
Manufacturers pay a fine for producing excess packaging. The money earned goes to recyclers.

Green Mark
Zero-waste products and services are labeled with a Green Mark so consumers can choose.

Household partners
Taiwan created a complex recovery system for capturing household waste. They collect 30 different kinds of waste and recycling twice a week, including fluorescent tubes and clothing.

Waste resources
Seventy-five percent of food waste turns into pig feed. Trashed furniture is fixed and donated to those who need it. Waste-to-energy incinerators create electricity.

Live a successful life: guaranteed!

Have you seen an advertisement like this before? Buy this new thing! Guaranteed to improve your life!

We're promised that the thing will make us smarter or more beautiful or more successful. But things are just things.

Maybe you are becoming a consumer for the first time in your life. (Hello, allowance! Hello, job!) What if buying something also meant picturing its end? How long will it last in a landfill?

SUPPLY & DEMAND: STUFF!

Demand: What We Want	Supply: How We Buy It	Big + Small Waste Solutions for Now + the Future
Water	In excess ... from our taps or in bottles	No wastewater will be wasted. It will be filtered, treated and reused at home.
Food	In excess ... from stores after it travels huge distances	We eat what we buy, and compost whatever is left.
Clothing	In excess ... from stores that want us to follow trends	Use fabrics that require less fertilizers, pesticides and water. Buy less!
Paper	In excess ... from stores (is there a trend here?)	Buy things that require less paper packaging.
Plastic	In excess ... from stores (you get it)	Look for the number. Buy the kind of plastic that gets recycled in your area. Reuse containers.
Glass	In excess ... from stores to use as containers	Undamaged glass can be used forever. Keep those containers and refill them from a bulk store.
Metal	In excess ... from stores that sell cans and foil-wrapped snacks	Recycle that can every time! Use a reusable drink bottle when possible.
Electronics	In excess ... from stores that want us to upgrade	Support safe e-recyclers.

GLOSSARY

aerate: to circulate air through a liquid or substance

alloy: a metal made by combining two or more metallic elements to build strength or prevent corrosion

anaerobic: without air. In anaerobic digestion, biodegradable materials break down in an oxygen-free environment.

aquifer: an underground layer of rock that can contain and move water

biodegrade: when a substance decomposes through the action of bacteria or another living organism

biogas: a fuel (usually methane) produced by the fermentation of organic matter

bioplastic: a type of plastic made from biological (living) substances rather than oil

black water: the water that gets flushed down the toilet

carbon footprint: a measure of the greenhouse gases produced by creating and using a service or product. A car has a larger carbon footprint than a bicycle.

cellulose: fibers from the bark, wood or leaves of plants

chemical elements: certain atoms with specific characteristics make up the basic chemical elements. For example, the chemical elements of carbon dioxide (CO_2) are carbon (C) and oxygen (O).

closed-loop system: a production process and life cycle that is designed to extend a product's life as much as possible by recovery, reuse or recycling. The goal is zero waste.

CO_2e: stands for *carbon dioxide equivalent* and is a unit for measuring carbon footprints

compost: decayed organic matter used for fertilizer

condensation: in the water cycle, when water vapor in the air rises, collects as clouds and then turns back into a liquid

decomposition: when organic substances are broken down into smaller bits of matter

deforestation: removing trees by cutting or burning them to use the land for another purpose

de-inking: the process of removing ink

desalination: the process of removing salt and minerals from sea water to make drinking water

digester: a container where substances are broken down into separate elements by heat or other processes. In wastewater processing, the digester is a giant tank where bacteria feast on sludge and break it down into methane, carbon dioxide and water.

downcycling: when waste is recycled and turned into something of lesser quality than the original product (like recycled paper)

effluent: liquid waste or sewage

enteric fermentation: the part of the digestive process of animals, such as cows, that causes them to emit methane gas

evaporation: in the water cycle, when the sun heats up surface and groundwater and turns it into water vapor

export: to send services or goods to another country for sale

fermentation: the chemical breakdown of a substance by bacteria, yeast or other microbes

foodprint: a combination of water footprint and carbon footprint that measures the environmental impact of food

fossil fuels: fuels like oil, natural gas and coal that are formed from the remains of organisms that lived a long time ago (fossils)

fracking: a system of injecting liquid into rocks with force to extract oil or gas

global warming: the gradual increase in Earth's atmospheric temperature

gray water: wastewater created from washing dishes, bathing and laundry

greenhouse gas: a gas that absorbs radiation and radiates heat. Greenhouse gases are a cause of global warming.

groundwater: water found underground in the spaces within sand, soil and rock

import: to bring in services or goods from another country

kWh: a unit for measuring and billing energy use that equals a kilowatt-hour of energy

landfill: where waste is dumped, buried and covered over with layers of soil and more waste. Landfills are the oldest method of waste disposal.

methane (CH_4): a gas used for fuel. It is the main component of natural gas. Some sources are organic waste decomposition, fossil fuel extraction and anaerobic digestion.

microbe: a microscopic organism; that is, a living thing too small to see without a microscope. Microbes may cause disease or fermentation.

NASA (National Aeronautics and Space Administration): the U.S. government office in charge of the science and technology behind airplane and space travel

open-loop system: a production process and life cycle that creates waste or, like downcycling, converts a product into a new, lesser-quality product

ore: a material from which a valuable metal or mineral can be extracted

polymer: a large molecule of repeating units

potable water: drinking water

precipitation: when water vapor in the sky forms droplets and is released as rain, snow, sleet or hail

pulp: a mixture of cellulose fibers separated from wood; a key ingredient in paper

reservoir: a storage space for fluids; also the underground area where crude oil is found

respirometry: a scientific test that measures decomposition by measuring respiration (the amount of CO_2 released)

reverse osmosis: the process through which solids (like salt) are removed from a solution (like water)

saline: containing salt

smelting: extracting a metal from ore by heating and melting

surface water: the water that collects on the surface of the ground

sustainable living: a way of living that considers the health of people and the planet when making or using something

synthetic: made by humans, often by chemical means, and usually meant to copy a natural product

thermal energy: energy that comes from heat

ton(s): in this book we have used tons, an imperial measure that means 2000 lb. (907 kg). A metric tonne is 1000 kg (2205 lb.).

transpiration: in the water cycle, when plants absorb water through their roots and give off water vapor through their leaves

waste audit: an assignment to collect, sort and weigh your waste

water footprint: a measure of the amount of water used to create or use something

zero waste: a goal for all waste to become a resource for another use

INDEX

FOR MORE INFORMATION

... about Water Waste

Visit

www.water.org
www.waterfootprintnetwork.org
www.watereducation.org

Read

One Well: The Story of Water on Earth, by Rochelle Strauss and Rosemary Woods. Toronto: Kids Can Press, 2007.

Water 4.0: The Past, Present, and Future of the World's Most Vital Resource, by David Sedlak. New Haven: Yale University Press, 2014.

Listen to

CBC Radio's *What a Waste*, "The Truth about Water Waste."
www.cbc.ca/whatawaste

... about Food Waste

Visit

www.cafeteriaculture.org
www.tristramstuart.co.uk

Listen to

CBC Radio's *What a Waste*, "Food Waste."
www.cbc.ca/whatawaste

Watch

Just Eat It: A Food Waste Story, by Grant Baldwin, 2014.
www.foodwastemovie.com

... about Clothing Waste

Visit

www.fashiontakesaction.com

Read

Overdressed: The Shockingly High Cost of Cheap Fashion, by Elizabeth Cline. New York: Portfolio/Penguin, 2012.

Watch

Fault Lines: Made in Bangladesh, by Al Jazeera, 2013.

Grow Your Own Clothes, TED Talk by Suzanne Lee, 2011.
www.ted.com/talks/Suzanne_lee_grow_your_own_clothes

The Next Black, by David Dworsky and Victor Kohler, 2014.

The True Cost, by Andrew Morgan, 2015.
www.truecostmovie.com

... about Paper Waste

Visit

www.ecology.com
www.recycling-guide.org.uk/science-paper.html

Listen to

Public Radio International (PRI)'s *Science Friday*, "Here Are All Your Burning Questions About Recycling, Answered."
www.pri.org/stories/2016-08-01/here-are-all-your-burning-questions-about-recycling-answered

... about Plastic Waste

Visit

www.environmentalhealthnews.org
www.recycleyourplastics.org

Read

Plastic-Free: How I Kicked the Plastic Habit and How You Can Too, by Beth Terry. New York: Skyhorse, 2012.

Watch

The Economic Injustice of Plastic, TED Talk by Van Jones, 2011.
www.ted.com/talks/van_jones_the_economic_injustice_of_plastic

... about Metal Waste

Visit

www.phys.org
www.sciencedaily.com
www.sciencekids.co.nz

Read

National Geographic Kids: Everything Rocks and Minerals, by Steve Tomecek. Washington, DC: National Geographic Children's Books, 2011.

... about E-Waste

Visit

www.ban.org (Basel Action Network)

Listen to

CBC Radio's *What a Waste*, "eWaste."
www.cbc.ca/whatawaste

Watch

The Story of Electronics, by Annie Leonard, Jonah Sachs and Louis Fox, 2011.
www.storyofstuff.org/movies/story-of-electronics

... about Space Waste

Visit

www.nasa.gov

Listen to

CBC Radio's *What a Waste*, "Space Junk."
www.cbc.ca/whatawaste

... about the Environment and Consumerism

Visit

www.davidsuzuki.org
www.epa.gov (United States Environmental Protection Agency)
www.greenschools.net
www.mnn.com (Mother Nature Network)
www.nationalgeographic.org/education
www.nrdc.org (National Resources Defense Council)
www.scientificamerican.com
www.smithsonianmag.com
www.worldwildlife.org

Read

Eyes Wide Open: Going Behind the Environmental Headlines, by Paul Fleischman. Somerville: Candlewick Press, 2014.

Garbology: Our Dirty Love Affair with Trash, by Edward Humes. New York: Avery, 2012.

Get Real: What Kind of World Are YOU Buying? by Mara Rockliff. Philadelphia: Running Press, 2010.

Zero Waste Home: The Ultimate Guide to Simplifying Your Life by Reducing Your Waste, by Bea Johnson. New York: Scribner, 2013.

Watch

The Story of Stuff, by Annie Leonard, Louis Fox and Jonah Sachs, 2007.
www.storyofstuff.org/movies/story-of-stuff